PROLOGUE

April 2017

YOU
DESERVE
BETTER

YOU
DESERVE
BETTER

What Life Has Taught Me About Love,
Relationships, and Becoming Your Best Self

TYLER CAMERON

PLUME

PLUME

An imprint of Penguin Random House LLC
penguinrandomhouse.com

Copyright © 2021 by Tyler Cameron
Penguin supports copyright. Copyright fuels creativity, encourages diverse voices,
promotes free speech, and creates a vibrant culture. Thank you for buying an authorized
edition of this book and for complying with copyright laws by not reproducing, scanning,
or distributing any part of it in any form without permission. You are supporting
writers and allowing Penguin to continue to publish books for every reader.

PLUME is a registered trademark and the P colophon is a trademark of
Penguin Random House LLC.

LIBRARY OF CONGRESS CATALOGING-IN-PUBLICATION DATA

Names: Cameron, Tyler, author.
Title: You deserve better : what life has taught me about love,
relationships, and becoming your best self / Tyler Cameron.
Description: [New York] : Plume, [2021] | Identifiers: LCCN 2021006112 (print) |
LCCN 2021006113 (ebook) | ISBN 9780593183564 (hardcover) |
ISBN 9780593183588 (ebook other)
Subjects: LCSH: Cameron, Tyler. | *Bachelorette* (Television program) |
Television personalities—United States—Biography. |
Self-actualization (Psychology) | Interpersonal relations.
Classification: LCC PN1992.4.C234 A3 2021 (print) |
LCC PN1992.4.C234 (ebook) | DDC 791.4502/8092 [B]—dc23
LC record available at https://lccn.loc.gov/2021006112
LC ebook record available at https://lccn.loc.gov/2021006113

Printed in the United States of America
1st Printing

BOOK DESIGN BY ALISON CNOCKAERT

*This book is dedicated to my momma. (I've spelled it
wrong since seventh grade, but you'll always be my momma.)*

*As I sit down to write this dedication, it's one day before the
one-year anniversary of your accident. Since you've passed away,
our lives have changed drastically. It's been a year of growth; it's been
a year of pain; it's been a year of joy as well. It's been very humbling.
Without all you've done the past twenty-seven years, and even this
last year, I wouldn't be able to do what I'm doing today.*

*This is dedicated to you for giving me, Austin, and Ryan—
and everyone in your life—your all. If all of us could be half as
loving as you were, the world would be a much better place.*

Love you and see you on the other side.

Contents

· · · · · · · · · · · · · · ·

Prologue   1

1. LESSONS FROM MY PARENTS: *Where I Come From*   15

The Real Tyler: According to His Dad, Jeff   29

2. A BRIEF HISTORY OF MY PAST RELATIONSHIPS:
    Learning Accountability   33

The Real Tyler: According to His Friend Mollie   57

3. MY FIRST LOVE: *What I Learned from Playing Sports*   63

The Real Tyler: According to His High School
    Guidance Counselor, Mrs. P   83

4. TAKE A CHANCE: *My Time on* The Bachelorette   87

The Real Tyler: According to His Friend Matt   109

5. BE RESPECTFUL: *How I Became an Accidental Feminist Icon*   115

• PSA FOR ALL MEN   131

CONTENTS

The Real Tyler: According to His Brother Ryan   135

6. BEING GOOD, DOING GOOD, FEELING GOOD:
   How I Found Myself (and My Selflessness)   139

   • BUILD YOUR TEAM: Lessons from My Mentors   153

7. DATING DOS AND DON'TS: *Red Flags and Green Lights*   169

   • A WORD ON ROMANCE   193

8. FEMALE FRIENDS AND BROMANCES:
   The Importance of Friendship   197

The Real Tyler: According to His Friend Katie   211

9. WHAT I'VE LEARNED FROM REJECTION:
   That Time I Got Broken Up with on National Television   217

The Real Tyler: According to His Friend and Mentor Robb   231

10. ALWAYS BE YOURSELF: *What Fame Has Taught Me*   235

The Real Tyler: According to His Brother Austin   251

11. A LETTER TO MY YOUNGER BROTHERS   255

Questions & Answers   261

Acknowledgments   273

YOU
DESERVE
BETTER

Holy shit, how did I end up here?

I'm somewhere in the middle of West Texas, miles from anyone or anything. For hours, I've just been driving, with no real destination, while my dad sleeps in the passenger seat next to me. Around us there's nothing but desert—just sand and sky for as far as I can see.

I can't believe how much things can change in twenty-four hours. Yesterday, I was strapping up my helmet and pads and hitting my last practice before the final game of the Spring League. Everything seemed fine with my girlfriend, Mariah. All I needed was one more good game to receive an invite for the start of NFL training camp. Then, during my first play of that last game, I dislocated my left shoulder—my good shoulder. It started out okay; I caught the ball, I hit the cornerback, I got the yardage. Then some dude came around the side of me and slung me down to the ground. When I fell, I landed on my shoulder and it popped right out of place. I'd had injuries before, but never like this, at such a critical moment. In an instant my football career, the thing I had dedicated so much of my life and energy to, was over.

My dad had been sick but came to Austin to see me play. As soon as the game wrapped, Pop looked at me sulking off the field and said, "Let's drive." We both knew my hopes of an NFL career were over. And just like that, we hit the road. That's how I came to find myself here. Wherever *here* even is.

I can barely lift my arm over the steering wheel, but by this point in my life, I've had so many shoulder issues because of football injuries that I barely notice the pain. I was raised according to my pop's philosophy: "You go to the hospital when you're dying." I can tell this shoulder injury isn't good, but it isn't an emergency, so for better or worse, I'm not going to pay it much mind.

My dad is making me do most of the driving. He's had some health issues in recent years, so he can't move around well, and he isn't much for driving anyway. He's slept most of the way since we left Austin, so I've been alone with my thoughts for a few hundred miles. I think about football, about my relationship, about my future, which in this moment feels like it's over before it's even begun. I think of all the ways I've messed up. I've rarely had cell service, but when I do, I try to call Mariah. She doesn't answer. I can't process that our relationship might be over, too.

I drive west for hours, until we find a place we can spend the night. It's not much of a town, really, just a tiny hotel and a gas station, surrounded by miles of nothing.

In the hotel room, on an uncomfortable bed, I don't sleep much. I wake up feeling defeated—about my arm, about my relationship, about my football career being over. Up until this point, my whole identity—my whole life, really—has been defined by football. My high school and college experiences, the friends I kept, the way I spent my free time—all of it orbited around football. For as long as I can remember, I've always been "T.C., the quarterback" or "T.C., the star athlete." If I don't have that anymore, then who the hell am I?

I head out to the hotel parking lot and sit down on one of those little bumpers they put at the end of a parking spot. As I'm sitting there, waiting for my dad to finish getting ready, Mariah calls me on FaceTime. She hasn't spoken to me at all since the game, ignoring my texts and calls for more than a day. Knowing something is wrong as I pick up my phone, I brace myself for a hard conversation. But when I see her face on the screen, I can tell it's worse than I thought.

"Tyler, I can't do this anymore." It's the first thing she says.

I'm speechless.

"You're not being a good boyfriend."

I try to think of a way to respond. But I'm so tired from the drive and a horrible night's sleep, and I'm so upset about my shoulder, that I just stay quiet. The simple truth is: She's right. I'm not. And I know it. For a long time leading up to this, I've been a terrible boyfriend to her. I've been immature, and I haven't dedicated myself to the relationship in the same way she has. For the last few months, I've been treating her wrong, talking shit to my buddies about our relationship, looking at other girls on social media, not putting energy into her or giving her support. She deserves so much better than what I have been giving. And yet, this moment still comes as a shock. A devastating one.

She dumps me, right there on FaceTime while I'm sitting on the ground in a parking lot in the middle of nowhere. When I hang up the phone, I feel like I've been beaten up—now emotionally as well as physically. I look up at the little two-story hotel where we're staying and feel a knot rising in my throat. All I want is to go home and go to bed, to put a blanket over my head and never come out. But instead, I'm stuck driving through the middle of Texas with my dad, on a road trip to absolutely nowhere.

When we get into the car, I tell him what happened. He starts to laugh.

"Well, you got me beat, son," he says. "The Dolphins cut me on a Wednesday, and my girlfriend cut me on a Friday. At least I had two days to recover. But you got hurt and then dumped the very next morning!" I've heard the story before, but now it hits home a little more than it used to. The parallel is so striking; I can see why he's laughing.

After a few miles on the highway, my dad falls asleep (again) and stays that way for most of the drive. From Austin, where we started our trip, it takes us nine hours to get out of Texas. I spend most of that time trapped in my own head.

How can I get Mariah back?

Where did it go wrong?

Who am I if I can't play football?

How did I get here?

What the hell am I going to do with my life?

I get deeper and deeper in my thoughts. As we drive, farther and farther west, I am more miserable than I've ever been.

Our first stop outside Texas is White Sands, New Mexico. I put on a brave face. I take pictures and post them on my social media, trying to pretend everything is okay. But the truth is, I'm completely heartbroken. I need advice on how to move forward. My dad and I don't talk much about relationships, this one with Mariah included.

I'm the oldest of three brothers, and since my dad and I don't usually get too deep in our conversations, I've never had a built-in role model to ask these kinds of questions. From a young age I learned to keep my feelings to myself and figure things out on my own.

We drive across New Mexico, through Arizona, all across the Southwest. It's the ideal road trip. The drive through this part of the country is gorgeous, but I'm not able to enjoy myself. The landscape is beautiful, some of the most stunning scenes you could imagine, but it's like I can't really see it. My mind isn't there.

Every night, I call Mariah and beg her to talk to me, to take me back, to give me another chance. Every night, she says, "No, Tyler. I can't." It goes on this way for a week.

Finally, my dad and I arrive in Utah. I've already been here—I had visited once the year before. On both occasions, the scenery takes my breath away. The bright rock formations belong more on Mars than on Earth, and the sky is just so *big*. My dad hasn't been anywhere out west before, so the whole trip I've been telling him, "We gotta go here. You've gotta see this. You're not going to believe it." Our final stop is Zion National Park, which might be the most beautiful place in the country. It's the most stunning place I've ever seen, at least.

I come from Florida, which is beautiful in its own way, but it's nothing but flat. Completely flat. (The closest thing we've got to a mountain is a garbage dump.) You've got your blue waters and your green trees; its beaches are the best in the world. But it's truly nothing compared to the awe-striking beauty in the West. The whole landscape is so bright and clear, and the scale is absolutely massive. There are mountain faces bigger than whole cities, and wide-open skies. You've got your blues and greens, but you've also got your reds and oranges, and every color in between. It's breathtaking, like nothing else I've ever seen in my life.

Once we get into the park, my dad hangs back on the ground while I decide to hike Angels Landing, which is considered to be one of the hardest hikes in America. With a really steep drop-off, it's also one of the scariest. Now is as good a time as any to mention that I'm deathly afraid of heights. I'm the biggest wimp; I can't handle them at all. But the scenery is so captivating and beautiful that I can't resist the promise of the view from the very top. To be fair, it's more out of ignorance than bravery that I decide to hike it. At this point I don't fully realize how high this route will take us or how narrow the path becomes in some places. Something else I don't yet know? This is about to be one of the most pivotal moments of my life.

I hadn't understood how steep this hike would be, but once I start climbing, it's too late to go back. For a lot of the time, there's no real trail, which makes it even scarier. With every step I take, I'm more anxious about how high up I am. I'm profusely sweating; I'm breaking out in hives. Every few seconds, I think, *I can't do this. I should turn around. I have to go back.* But the higher up I get, the more incredible the view becomes. And so, maybe foolishly, I push on.

My progress is slow, and I'm still freaking out, so I decide to take a break. I start chatting with this guy who looks like he knows what he's doing.

"How much farther up?" I ask him.

He says we still have hours to go, a fact that he seems excited about. All I can think is, *Oh great.* I tell him I'm from Jupiter, Florida. He can't believe it.

"One of my buddies is from Jupiter!" he says. "He's farther up the mountain."

It's so random—Jupiter is not a big town—that I figure it must be a sign. I keep on rolling.

When I get higher up the mountain, I meet the guy's friend, and he recognizes me. It turns out he's my aunt's next-door neighbor, and we instantly hit it off. It's a strange coincidence, and it immediately makes me feel more comfortable, like I'm not alone. I decide to follow his group, tailing them as we head up, higher and higher. They're sailing up the mountain, and I'm barely keeping up. I'm totally drenched with sweat, from both the hike and my nerves. I feel like they're skipping as I'm crawling, but still, it's great to have something to keep me going.

At this point, I learn two lessons. The first is that if you want to go fast, go alone; if you want to go far, find someone to go with you. Having other people there doesn't just help me face my fear of heights but also gives me the support and motivation I need to keep going.

The second lesson I learn is that if I want to make it all the way to the top, the only way to get there is to just focus on taking one step at a time. Whenever I look off to the side of the trail and see how far it is to the ground, I immediately panic. If I so much as glance beyond my path, I start shaking.

So, because I have no real choice, I keep my head down. I don't let myself get distracted. With each step, I think to myself, *The next good thing, the next good thing, the next good thing.* This becomes a mantra I always carry with me. If I keep my head down and put one foot in front of the other, both literally and metaphorically, I'll get where I need to go. No matter what you want to accomplish, the more you focus on each small, good thing, the more good things will follow.

With every step I take, I feel my confidence building.

I know it sounds cheesy, but my life changes on my way up that mountain.

At the foot of the trail, I had never felt more broken and lonely. But by the end, I'm a different person. When I finally make it to the top of the mountain, I feel strong, like I've accomplished the impossible and overcome a real fear. It's not that the hike itself is such a big deal (although, to me, it was)—people make that climb every day. It's that I've taken a monumental step in believing in myself. If I can do this, I realize, then I can do anything. Just by taking it step by step, putting one foot in front of the other.

At the top of the mountain, I play this song, "Remedy," by Zac Brown Band. It's a beautiful song, about how you get what you give:

I've been thinking about the mark that I'll be leaving
Been looking for a truth I can believe in . . .

As I look down, my first thought is, *Holy shit. I'm up here. I made it.*

My second thought is how incredibly gorgeous everything is. I can see the giant bus I arrived on that carries tourists around the park. On the ground it was huge, but from up here I have to squint to make it out. As I scan the park and take in the epic scale of the scenery around me, it makes me appreciate how big the world really is and how small we really are. All my problems, which seemed so huge back on the ground, suddenly feel so little. Sometimes, that perspective shift is all you need.

I stay up there for three full hours, taking it all in. At one point, I feed a chipmunk some nuts from my backpack, like something out of a Disney movie. (This seriously happened. At Zion, the chipmunks are so fat, because everyone feeds them. Which I guess you're not supposed to do. But I digress.)

I know in my heart that I was meant to go on this hike. I needed something to make me want to keep going. I was in the dumps. I was feeling so hurt, so lost, so empty, but now this accomplishment has given me that feeling like there is something more to this life. It's given me a shot of confidence when I sorely need it. I force myself to realize that I'm more than just a football player. My value isn't determined by the mistakes I've made or what I have or haven't done yet. I have a lot more to give, and from this moment forward, I'm going to do better.

· · · · ·

The road trip with my dad lasts for fourteen days.

From then on, the number fourteen haunts me. For a while, it seemed like everything happened on the fourteenth of the month.

On April 14, 2017, my dad and I started the road trip.

Almost a year later, on February 14, I got the call that I had been cast on *The Bachelorette*.

On March 14, I left for the show.

On May 14, I came back home.

I couldn't help but notice. Whenever a pattern or a coincidence pops up, I always pay attention, because you never know where it can lead you. I do believe in signs. I believe that sometimes things happen for a reason, sometimes things feel meant to be, sometimes there's a greater force acting behind the smallest details. I think in life, there's a voice, or an instinct, or just a gut feeling that tells us there's more, something bigger at play. You don't always know the reason why. You may not even notice until way after the fact. But it's important to pay attention to what the signs are telling you and to be open to letting them guide your path.

My dad tells a story that illustrates this point. When he was twenty-one, he was home from college and staying at his girlfriend's house when he woke up at three o'clock in the morning with a feeling that he had to go home no matter what. He had no idea why he woke up or why he had this overwhelming urge to rush back to his house, but he did. When he got there, he discovered his mom walking out the door. She told him she wasn't feeling well and was on her way to the hospital. She died the next day.

Sometimes, when something like that hits you, you don't always understand it in the moment, but you have to pay attention to your feelings and the way things impact you as they're happening. If something feels significant, even if you can't understand why or how it could be, you've got to trust that instinct. That's the feeling I got when I finished that hike. I just knew that it mattered somehow. It was a huge change in perspective and mind-set exactly when I needed it.

Each day, I think about that hike as I get up and put one foot in front of the other. I'm still learning, still trying to reach that undiscovered peak in the clouds. But I've come to recognize that that's okay; that's what life is. It's all an unknown. Even when you reach your goal, you get a glimpse of the beautiful view around you, and then you discover that there's still more ahead. You're going to have to keep on climbing.

What I learned is to just focus on the next step—the next class, the next job, the next show, the next date, whatever it is. Approaching any challenge, or making any change in your life, can be as simple as hiking that mountain became for me, if you just keep putting one foot in front of the other.

More than anything, that experience taught me that, over and over again, we find ourselves in situations where we don't think we can succeed. Whenever I fuck up, it's because I looked off to the side and got distracted or psyched myself out. Sometimes those big dreams, those overall goals, are scary. That's because when you dream of the future, looking at the big picture can seem intimidating, can make you think you have to aim lower. But by taking on that challenge one small step at a time, anything is within reach.

I learned a lot that day, clearly, but it was only the beginning. I've learned a lot more since. I've learned that I deserve more from myself, that I owe it to myself to consistently try my best. I've learned the importance of surrounding myself with the right people and giving back more than I take. I learned that rejection isn't the worst thing. And I learned that as long as I give it my all, I can live without regrets.

I definitely don't have all the answers, and I'm learning more every day. But one thing I know for sure is that all of us have value and all of us are worthy of being treated equally and with respect. If you're struggling to believe in yourself or to find your way, trust me when I say that I've been there. If you're looking to break down toxic masculinity and take responsibility for your actions, I've been there. If you're ready to find love and learn how to give value to another person, I've been there, too. These are some stories from my own life and the lessons they've taught me. Whether you're currently at your rock bottom or looking down from the top of a mountain, I hope you'll keep reading. Because you deserve the best, from yourself, your life, and your relationships. I hope I can show you what that means to me, so you can try to find it for yourself.

1

LESSONS FROM MY PARENTS

Where I Come From

For better or worse, the relationships we see as we're growing up shape our ideas about love. Those early models can sometimes pave the way for the relationships we have (or don't have) in the future. And I, like so many people, didn't have a model relationship to learn from. My parents dedicated their lives to raising three great children, but when it came to their own marriage, they had a rocky, uneven partnership. When Shakespeare wrote, "The course of true love never did run smooth," he might as well have been talking about them.

Growing up, I had a mom who loved me, a dad who loved me, and two parents who loved each other. But their ways of showing their love for each other were not always healthy—not for them, or for us kids, who witnessed it. They were oil and water, and they feuded constantly. Watching their relationship, which was both unhealthy and yet based in love, gave me a very confusing image of what a loving relationship should look like.

Perhaps the biggest reason I haven't had many long-term relationships is because, for much of my young life, I didn't see a relationship that I wanted for myself. When you don't have any positive role models for what a healthy relationship looks like, it can be easy to fall into a bad one, to imitate patterns, or, what seemed like the easiest option for me, to avoid having relationships altogether. For a long time, I struggled—and sometimes still struggle—to understand what a solid relationship should look like. Eventually, I found role models whose relationships I could look up to. But for a long time, in a lot of ways, I had to figure that one out on my own.

That's not to say I didn't learn from watching my parents. I did; in fact, I learned a lot. They taught me the power of hard work, helping others, and never giving up. But as far as relationships are concerned, they taught me everything I didn't want to be.

My parents actually split up twice. The first time they separated, I was two years old. Even though I was a toddler, I have some memories from that time. Mostly I remember them fighting about things I didn't understand. Even though I was too young to fully grasp what was happening, that situation caused me stress. When I got older and thought about it, I knew I never wanted to put my own kids in a situation like that. My mom and I moved four streets away, and for a time, we lived apart from my dad.

Eventually, my dad bought this beautiful house on the water and said he would do whatever it took to get his family back. When I was around four years old, my parents got back together and had two more kids, my younger brothers, Austin and Ryan. We all lived in that house together, and for a while, it was paradise. Ours was the most happening, fun home there was. It was on a peninsula, with three-quarters of the property surrounded by water. Every Thursday through Sunday, it was the party house. Friends would come over, and we would all be together, partying and cooking out. It was so family-friendly. I remember how it felt—like we had nothing to worry about. We stayed there for nine happy years.

But then when the housing market crashed in 2008, my dad, who was a builder, lost the house, along with everything else he had. (For a long time, my dream was to buy it back someday. But sadly, it was recently torn down.) After that, things got really rough. The second time my parents split, I was fifteen or sixteen. That time, it would be for good.

Even when they were together, though, my parents weren't models for a healthy relationship. For starters, in the past, my dad suffered from alcoholism and depression. He's now in recovery, but when I was a kid, he would sometimes turn to alcohol when times were hard. He always supported us financially, but he wasn't there for emotional support, for us or for Mom. There are some things that, for everyone's sake, I'd rather not discuss in detail. But may it suffice to say that I've lived and felt things that I hope my kids will never have to experience.

My parents put my brothers and me through some difficult stuff, but I know we're not the only family to live this story. These can be challenging and consuming situations. Some people have to cut off contact with family members if this type of behavior goes on for too long; I can understand that choice. But for me, I'll never stop being my dad's son. I stand by his side because I also see his whole story. My dad had a hard life. He never had a father, he lost his mom at twenty-one, and then he lost his brother at twenty-five. Everything he did in life, from his school to his job to his family, was something he had to figure out on his own. It's not an excuse for his actions, but

I have a lot of sympathy for him. There were plenty of times when I wanted to say, "Fuck it," and cut him out of my life. But in the end, he had an awakening and saw that he needed to get his shit together, and I'm glad that he did. Thankfully for us, for our family, it turned out okay.

As I've gotten older, one thing that scares me is realizing how much our lives are all about perspective. So much of who we are and who we become boils down to how we look at things and what we take from any given situation. My perception of my parents' relationship, and of our family as a whole, is so different from my brothers' perceptions, because I'm the oldest and things happened at different stages of our development. Sometimes I fear they'll fall into the same patterns my parents did or be afraid of relationships, even more than I have been. Being a role model for them is something I am constantly striving for.

My parents would both tell me negative stories about the other one to try to get me to take sides. In high school, I took my mom's side. She was like my best friend, because at the time she was the one who was always there for me. I was the star quarterback, and she was the mom who brought a fresh foot-long sub to my practice every day. But when I went to college, I started to side with my dad. I'd come home from school and see my brothers eating boxed mac 'n' cheese while she was gone somewhere, and I would fault her for not giving them the same attention she had once given me. But I see now that wasn't fair of me, and it wasn't the whole picture. I didn't see the struggles my mom went through. I didn't understand that she just wanted love and support, too. She wanted to be treated the way she deserved to be treated. My dad worked hard to support everyone financially, but my mom wanted a partner who would share the responsibilities of raising a family, too. She always said, "He paid all the bills, but he never paid the attention bill."

When we had the house on the water, my mom was the coolest girl on the block. She was a social butterfly, making tons of friends and getting the attention she always loved. Once we lost the house, she still craved that social interaction, but she needed to find it elsewhere. She started dating and had a few boyfriends once she and my dad were done. This new lifestyle choice was hard for me to accept at the time. I remember one time, when I was in college, I wanted to physically fight one of her boyfriends. He wasn't my dad, and I didn't get how she could be with anyone else. But it's weird how sometimes little things can hit you and change your perspective. The first time I heard the lyrics to a Drake song, where he asks, "Who the fuck wants to be seventy and alone?" I was like, *Oh shit*. I got it. My mom was only after what we all want. She just wanted someone to care about her.

After that point, I eased into accepting her boyfriend, Pauly. Eventually, I came to love the guy. They were together for eight years, and that was one of the first times I saw a healthy relationship in action. They took care of each other, and their relationship was built on trust and respect. I had never seen my mom happier. That helped me start to understand that romantic love can function in a positive, healthy way.

Even after seeing what a healthy relationship looked like, I didn't completely understand that my parents' relationship was toxic until I was out of college. Before that, I just figured everyone had their problems. I thought arguing was how people communicated. But as I grew up and gained a greater perspective, I saw how unhealthy and damaging that was.

· · · · ·

One night, a week before Christmas, I was getting ready to take my last exam to get my general contractor's license. I called my dad to check in on him, and he told me his stomach felt like it was on fire. As a precaution, I told my brother to take him to the hospital, but I didn't think too much of it. It's not that I didn't take him seriously; I'd just heard it a million times before.

The next morning, I called to let him know that I'd passed my exam and was going to be a general contractor, just like him. I discovered he was still in the hospital, and his condition had only gotten worse. "Something's not right," he said. I rushed there and stayed with him in the hospital for the next three days. The doctors couldn't figure out what was wrong with him. That was enough for him. The doctors were trying to help, but he felt like they weren't doing anything right. "Get me out of here," he told me. So we did as he asked and brought him home.

I sat by his open bedroom door all night, just watching him. He was really out of it. He couldn't eat; he would throw up everything. He couldn't really sleep. The next morning, he was weak and pale and barely looked alive. I carried him to the car and rushed him back to the hospital. They immediately brought him to the ICU and ran a battery of tests on him.

The doctors discovered he had an infection that was starting to go septic. He was in so much pain that they put him in an induced coma. The next step was to undergo emergency surgery. When the doctors split his gut, they discovered that his small intestine had wrapped and knotted together, causing a blockage, and a portion of it had to be cut out. Because he was in the coma, I was the person who needed to sign off on his rights, which was one of the hardest things I've ever had to do. I did my best to stay strong for my brothers, but no matter how hard I tried to fight it, I couldn't stop crying.

My dad says he remembers being wheeled down the hallway and seeing the signs for hospice and emergency surgery. As they wheeled him closer to surgery, he saw a bright light and thought it was taking him to die. He says he tried to fight it off. He told it over and over that he wasn't ready. Eventually, the light turned off.

My dad remained in that coma for twelve days.

During the daytime, I took over his business, keeping his construction projects running. I was already working on two different housing projects of my own, and with the addition of my dad's work, that number suddenly bumped up to ten. I spent my days acting like nothing was wrong and forging his signature to keep it all going. (Eventually, when he came to, we told everyone what was going on.)

Before my dad got sick, my parents did *not* like each other. They still had love for each other, but after their second split, they couldn't be in the same room together. They would immediately bicker; they didn't get along at all. But during my dad's health struggles, my parents got close again. My mom did so much to help out with my dad, and they became best friends again. It was the first time in my life, at least that I could remember, when everyone was fully there for one another. It was so nice to see my parents care for each other, and it made life so much better. We were finally able to do things as a family again.

After his time in the hospital, my dad didn't drink anymore. He promised to make a change, and he committed to taking care of himself. At first there were a couple of times when he still drank here and there, but I sat him down and said, "Dad, you can't." Thankfully, he took me seriously. Of course, he still has struggles. He will always have to fight his alcoholism, and like many of us, he suffers from periods of anxiety and depression. But I'm so proud of what he's been able to achieve, the strength he's shown to ultimately save his own life.

When I was twenty-six years old, for the first time since I was in eighth grade, we all spent Thanksgiving and Christmas together as a family. It was the most amazing thing, the realization of a dream I had always had for all of us to spend time together. That year we all had so much fun together. Pauly, my mom's longtime boyfriend, was there, and everyone got along. We spent Thanksgiving in New York City, even going to the Macy's Thanksgiving Day Parade. It felt like life had gotten to where it was supposed to be.

But life can be incredibly unexpected. For years, my biggest fear was speaking at my dad's funeral, and for good reason. I never expected that I would need to speak at my mom's.

Just a couple months after our holidays together, my mom unexpectedly passed away. It came as a huge blow to our entire family, something we're still learning to cope with. What I do know is that I am so grateful for that last year, where we got to do everything together and enjoy one another's company as a family. It was such a blessing that we were able to have that time together at the end. It felt like our relationships with one another had started to heal.

My parents had a hard, hard relationship. But I know that despite it all, even though they couldn't be together happily, my mom and my dad really loved each other. When they were married, they cared a lot about their relationship, but they had no idea how to express it, which I think is why they argued so much. They never poured themselves back into each other. At the end of the day, some people aren't meant for each other. No matter how much they try, sometimes it's just not possible to force compatibility.

My parents had a lot of struggles, but for me, there was one big takeaway. Over and over I observed that when things got hard between them, they didn't turn toward each other. When things broke down, they turned away and looked for support and solace outside their relationship—my mom sought out the attention of friends, my dad went looking for the bar. But that's not how to handle your issues. You can't run from them or ignore them. That only makes them bigger and bigger, worse and worse. If there's one thing I want to do differently than my parents, it's turning to my partner when we have an issue and then confronting it together. That way, we can keep on moving forward, knowing that we'll go further if we're climbing together. For me, I know "The One" will be the person I talk to when things are going perfectly *and* when things are going completely wrong.

· · · · ·

Because of my parents' relationship, I think, in some ways, my heart has been broken since I was a kid. That's probably part of why I watched and loved R&B videos so much when I was growing up, because they showed me this dream of romance that was everything I wanted. Of course, there were the classics, like "Here and Now" by Luther Vandross and Boyz II Men's "On Bended Knee." They talk about being faithful and making promises and never letting go. I still love those songs so much. It might sound a little strange, but without a strong relationship I could look to as a model in my real life, these songs were what first taught me what romance was. They helped me believe that things could be different between two people who loved each other.

My favorite artist was (and still is) the rapper Juice WRLD. I've listened to his songs after a lot of big moments in my life. His albums teach a lot about the trajectory of relationships. The first album is about heartbreak, the second one is about coming together, and the third one is about being in a good relationship and living that dream. In my life up to this point, I definitely relate to the heartbreak album the most. Sadly, I'm sure I'm not the only one who feels this way.

"I'm Still" is one of my favorite songs, and I think it sums up where I'm at right now:

I'm still flexin' with my heart broken
Got my heart open, I'm not high yet

My first heartbreak was because of my parents. But there are lessons in everything, and I've tried to learn what I can from them. For a long time, I wondered, *Why would I want to be in a relationship when they cause so much heartbreak?* But over time, I came around to the realization that not all relationships cause pain.

I still struggle with the idea of relationships. I worry that maybe I'm not enough. I worry that even if I find a good relationship, I'll fuck it up. But we all have to face our fears eventually, and I'm at an age and a place in my life where I can't make excuses for myself anymore. It can be scary, but I'm still putting myself out there, with the knowledge that I can do better than my parents did.

In the end, my parents taught me some positives about love. They showed me a lot about forgiveness, about redemption, about friendship, and about family. I've seen how treacherous love can be when it's mishandled and taken for granted. But I also know that anything good is worth fighting for. My heart is open, and I'm ready to try.

The Real Tyler:

....

ACCORDING TO HIS DAD, JEFF

I've been very fortunate. I've got three very good kids. I'm not an expert, and I'm no angel. Sometimes I look back and think, *Damn, maybe I was a little too hard on them.* Maybe I overdid it because I didn't have a father. The father-son dynamic can be a tough thing, because they want to hear it from everyone but you. But there are certain sayings we all live by, and certain core values I stressed on my kids.

When Tyler and his brothers were growing up, there was only one thing I never allowed. They could keep their rooms a little bit dirty; they didn't have to make straight A's . . . those things I could live with. But respect? That's the one thing where there was a solid line in the road. You respect me, you respect your mother, you respect any elder, you respect women. Real simple.

Tyler's dream—for his whole life, from the time he was a little kid—was to play pro football. So the one thing I always instilled in him was that besides talent, you've gotta work really hard. One thing

I say all the time is, "Be your best self every day." You can't change other people. The only thing you can control is yourself. Your goal should just be to be your best self every day. If you keep it that simple, life can be pretty easy. When Tyler tried to play pro ball, he didn't make it. But he did his best, so he was able to move on to the next chapter. If you do your best, you don't look back. That's all you can do.

When it comes to sports, and really to life in general, you've gotta outwork everybody. Tyler and I used to run these giant sand hills every day. We'd name them—we'd call one Clemson, we'd call one Florida State, we'd name them after the competition. I would drive him and his buddy down to the field every morning at 7:30 a.m., even though practice didn't start until 9:00. They would hop the chain-link fence and get to work. When you work that hard, you don't just develop your physical strength—you develop your mental strength as well. I think the mental piece is even more important than the physical one. When you know you've outworked everyone else, you start to see the world differently. You look down that field and you know you *deserve* to win.

I'll never forget it—after he got cut by the NFL, Tyler was home in Florida, working for me, and he was down and depressed. He walked up to me at work one day and said, "I got a call. They want to talk to me, for a TV show." I was like, "What the hell you talking about? What TV show?" He told me he'd filled out something to audition for *The Bachelorette*, and I said, "What the hell is *The Bachelorette*?" That's how much I knew.

I was like, "Is it going to cost you any money? If not, what do you have to lose?" So he took off work and went to do his interview. I didn't expect it to go any further than that. Then two weeks later, he's on the job, and he tells me he has to take off again because he has to go back for another interview.

That night, I plugged in my computer, and typed "What is Bachelorette?" When I saw everything that came up for it, I was like, "Whoa, this isn't little time; this is big time!"

When they first told Tyler that he got on the show, he didn't want to go. I was sick at the time, and he didn't want to leave. I said, "Son! This is Miss Alabama!" He would be a fool not to go and meet Hannah. With that Southern accent? She can tell you to take the garbage out and it sounds good! I told him, "If you don't go, I'm gonna go!"

After he left for the show, there was no contact for two and a half months, so I had no idea how things were going. When he came back for his hometown visit, that fool was ate up in love! I know my kid, and I'd never seen him like that.

• • • • •

We live in a small town, where everybody knows everyone else. When it came to Tyler, the kid played college football on TV every weekend, he was signed by the Ravens, he was getting up there. But when all that was going on, outside of my buddies, nobody really gave a shit. Then he got on that TV show, and it was like the pope was in town.

When the show first came on, a sports bar near our house hosted a watch party every Monday night. Every single TV in the bar would play *The Bachelorette*, and it was standing room only. Anywhere I went in the whole county, it was all I would hear about.

Ty, the whole town's watching, I would think. *I just hope you don't get cut on the first episode.* Then he got past the first couple of episodes, and I hoped he would stick around so he'd get to travel a bit. We never thought what happened would happen. It was like a weird strike of lightning. Tyler going on a show and getting famous was never in the plans. But it just goes to show you, when the lord closes one door, he opens a window. Tyler got cut from the NFL, and this whole new direction opened up for him—and it's better for him, because he's not getting beat up all the time!

Tyler is a great example of how you've got to find a purpose in life. Everybody's got a niche, and you need to find yours. I like to say that the lord gave us a set of cards. Figure out what they are, and play them wisely. When he was in high school, Tyler wanted to be a pro basketball player. So I got out the stats of every top recruit in the country, and we looked at them together. These guys were six seven, six eight, seven feet tall. I was like, "Tyler, you're six three. This just isn't your niche." But his niche was still out there. (And yours is, too. No matter what avenue you pick, whether you're a plumber, a lawyer, an electrician, a teacher—get up every day and be the best at what you do.)

When it comes to haters, I always say, don't feed the alligators. Don't acknowledge them. If you acknowledge them, they're getting what they want out of you. They're like a rotten fruit; instead of giving them water, just let them dry up. When you're at the top, you're always going to get haters. You can't listen to what anybody else says; you just have to be yourself. That's what Tyler is great at. He's always completely himself. He's not a good dancer, but he dances anyway, and he doesn't care. And I hope he inspires other people to be themselves, too. That's how everybody should be.

2

A BRIEF HISTORY OF MY PAST RELATIONSHIPS

Learning Accountability

It's safe to say my approach to relationships has changed *a lot* over the years. In my earliest relationships, I was, as the youths would call it, a simp. I was a total kiss-ass, a sweetheart. The truth is, when I'm in a relationship, I still turn that way; I'm a pretty lovey-dovey person. I'm a softy who loves all the romantic stuff—I can't help it. But back when I was in middle school, it was really over-the-top.

In seventh grade, I had my first girlfriend, Emily. Like many middle schoolers at that time, our relationship largely consisted of a lot of endless phone calls and a lot of big emotions. I would cry for hours, boo-hooing into the phone every night. I was so in love. At the time, I definitely thought she was the love of my life and that we were going to wind up together. It was a little naive, maybe, to think I would find the love of my life at thirteen, but I really did believe it. I acted like my life was a Ja Rule/Ashanti music video.

Growing up, my dad didn't want me dating at all because he

wanted me to focus on sports and not get distracted by girls. We got into some huge fights about it. Pretty much every night, he'd tell me to get off the phone: "You can't be crying all night again!" To which I'd reply, "NO! YOU DON'T KNOW WHAT LOVE IS!" Like I said, I was very dramatic.

When my mom and dad argued, which happened a lot, I'd take the phone and go hide somewhere in the house so I could talk to Emily until 4:00 a.m. Ours was a highly dramatic middle school relationship. We had all these intense emotions for each other, and then she'd break up with me on a whim. I'd have to fight to win her back, something that happened over and over. One time, I messed up (I don't remember how), so I brought her flowers. On the card I wrote, *I love you forever, babby.* I didn't even know how to spell the frickin' word *baby.* My teacher—who was also the mother of one of my friends—saw it and still makes fun of me about that to this day. Another time, that same teacher sent a student to go rescue me from the bathroom, where I was crying because Emily had dumped me yet again.

When Emily broke up with me for good, I was heartbroken. At the old age of thirteen, I decided I was done with relationships forever. That lasted all of two years.

I went to the biggest high school in Palm Beach County. It resembled the kind of high school that you would see on a Disney Channel show, where the kids all seemed happy, shiny, and beautiful, and everything was a ton of fun. Of course, cliques came with the territory of a big school like that. As the quarterback, I was automatically considered one of the cool kids. Even as a freshman I was a hotshot, which, for better or worse, made life at school feel pretty easy. Despite our history, Emily and I remained friends all along, and when we got to high school, she transitioned into the gorgeous, popular girl, straight out of a teen movie. The summer after my freshman year, we started seeing each other again.

One day, while my mom was out of town for the weekend, Emily came over to hang out. At that point, we had been dating again for a few months and both felt like we were totally in love. We were ready to take the next step in our relationship. My best friend Keddy was staying at our place that weekend, where he was sleeping in my room with me. My younger brother was sleeping in his room. Since both of the bedrooms were occupied, Emily and I needed somewhere else to go. The only other place in the house with any privacy was . . . my mom's room. Yes, this is the story of how I lost my virginity in my mom's bed.

So there we were, kissing in my mom's room, when I realized: *It's about to go down.* I was trying to be cool, but things kept happening to ruin the vibe. At one point, the cat jumped on the bed and started playing with Emily's hair. I had to move the cat out of the way like three times. Eventually, I had to stop what I was doing, stand up, and chase the cat out of the room. But then, finally, all distractions were gone.

And then, it was over. I didn't know what to do after, so I jumped up and said, "I'll be right back!" A few moments later, I came back to the room, all proud of myself, only to discover that Emily was gone. I found her in my mom's bathroom, crying. This was not how I'd pictured this going at all.

This is the point when I realized it was *her* virginity, too, which was news to me. In retrospect, we should have talked about all of this, but at the time, I didn't know better. (Now, before I get into bed with anyone, I ask about every possible thing. I always make sure everyone's intentions are clear and that both people are enthusiastic and comfortable with what's happening. But it would take me a minute to learn that.)

Emily stayed over that night and left early the next morning. Everything felt fine after the fact, but as soon as she left, the panic set in. *What if I've gotten her pregnant?* I didn't know what to do. I know now that communication is key, but instead of reaching out to her, I kept my feelings to myself.

The next day, I went fishing with my buddies, and the whole time, I was dead quiet. No one had any idea what was wrong with me. I was freaking myself out, spiraling deeper and deeper into this fear that Emily was pregnant. I didn't say anything to my friends; I didn't say anything to her. I remained quiet for days, worrying in my head, obsessing over this new fear. Eventually, she called me out over Facebook.

"How could you do this?" she wrote. "You hooked up with me and disappeared?!"

Of course she felt that way. That's exactly what it looked like to her. But I honestly wasn't ghosting her; I was just freaked out. I didn't know what to say; I didn't know how to talk about it. So I figured the best thing was to say nothing. Of course, from her perspective, that was the worst thing I could possibly do, but it would still be a while before I learned about healthy communication. Years later, I explained everything to her, and Emily and I are homies to this day, but looking back, I realize that my behavior really put our friendship, let alone our relationship, in jeopardy.

The bigger problem was that once I found out what sex was—once I discovered for myself that it was fun—I wanted to do it all the time. Hooking up was a huge thing at my high school. Everyone went to parties or hung out on the beach, where the expectation was to casually hook up. Hook-up culture defined my generation's high school and college experiences. Without parents teaching us something different, we didn't know better; we saw these things modeled on TV or in movies, and we thought that was just what you did. For a long time, I thought that was what being a boy was all about.

In high school, I had my second relationship with this other girl, Kelsey. I was so into her. That was the dream. We started dating in January, right around my birthday, and we had plans to hang out with each other for the big day. When my birthday rolled around, she said she had to study, so instead, I spent it at Miller's Ale House eating Capt. Jack's Buried Treasure (my favorite thing).

The next day, I found out the truth of where she had been the night before. I went to school to discover she had hickeys all over her neck. I didn't see the hickeys, but the whole school was gossiping about them. One of my boys saw her neck and asked, "Why'd you do that, bro? Why'd you give her all those hickeys? That's not cool." I had no idea what he was talking about, but I knew it had nothing to do with me. That's never been my thing. I mean, no shade if that's what you're into, but it's just not for me.

I found Kelsey in the hallway and said, "Let me see your neck."

She wouldn't show me. She stormed off instead.

As it turned out, I guess she did have to study . . . and then she hooked up with some guy at the library. And that was all I needed to know.

My relationship with Kelsey had started off as the teenage dream—"high school quarterback dates pretty cheerleader and lives happily ever after." It was basically a Taylor Swift song. Like I mentioned, I was taking my dating cues from pop culture, and movies of the early 2000s didn't always show the healthiest or most real versions of relationships. Dating Kelsey was exactly what I thought I wanted. But in reality, our relationship was short-lived, and when it ended, I became so disillusioned and felt so betrayed. I had gone all in—with my hopes and my feelings—only to watch the whole thing crash and burn.

It seemed like the easiest way to avoid being hurt by relationships was to stop being in one. After that, I quit dating altogether. Instead, I became the ultimate party boy. I spent so much time hanging out with my friends, my main focus just having a good time. It was fun, and a part of me enjoyed that lifestyle, but the truth is, I wasn't in it for the partying. The real reason I acted that way was because I didn't want to get rejected again. Relationships scared me. All I knew of them, both from what I'd seen at home and what I'd experienced in my own life, was that they caused pain. Why would I want that? If I partied and focused on football, it seemed like I got to have all the fun parts, with none of the heartbreak.

After high school, I headed to college at Wake Forest, a top twenty-five university, in Winston-Salem, North Carolina. From the moment I arrived, I kept up that party-boy attitude. I had fun, I hooked up with girls, and no relationship ever got beyond that. I never let myself get attached. I never got close to anyone.

Looking back on that time, it was *bad*. I was behaving really poorly, letting my own past heartbreak change the way I treated other people. I'm not proud of how I acted, and I feel like I wasn't acting with respect toward others or myself. I actually got black-listed from certain sororities because I hooked up with too many girls. There was an app called Yik Yak at the time, which was like an anonymous Twitter feed for students at universities. People would go on Yik Yak and report what went down the night before—what they did, what they saw, or what they heard other people had done. After a night of partying, my buddies and I would wake up and get on the Wake Forest Yik Yak to see what dirt got posted about us. There was usually a lot. It was a small school, and we were pretty well-known, being on the football team.

My entire time at Wake Forest was just party, party, party, football, football, football. My only identity back then was "Tyler, the football player," so I didn't put any effort into anything else. It was the same way people saw me in high school, as just a jock and not much else. My first semester at college, I got a 1.8 GPA. I'm not proud of that. Looking back I know I should have taken advantage of my time as a student. If I could do it over, my focus would have been on school (and maybe building up more meaningful relationships), but I was in a hurt place, and my wake-up call was still a ways off.

And yet, it wasn't all bad. I didn't realize it at the time, but in a way, Wake Forest turned my life around. It stopped a bad pattern from spiraling out of control. Back at my high school, everyone had casual sex like it was nothing. At fourteen or fifteen, people got fake IDs and started going to clubs. If that was what it was like in high school, you can imagine what happened for a lot of my classmates once they got to college. All these people from my hometown went to big party schools in Florida, where they kept up their wild lifestyles with the same people. They got into so much trouble, some of it serious.

Wake Forest, on the other hand, was a totally different scene. It's the kind of place where many of the students were the valedictorian of their high school. The girls all had their Tory Burch flats and pearls and always seemed to be on their best behavior. Everyone wore shorts over their bathing suits. Compared to my teenage years in Jupiter, I found that girls expected a lot more from guys before they were ready to talk about sex. I brought my party lifestyle with me, but I was a bit of an outlier. My friends would say things like, "T.C., you're wild!" or "T.C., you're crazy!" No one ever urged me to take it further. That slowed me down a lot.

When I transferred to Florida Atlantic University my junior year, the girls were the total opposite of what I'd experienced at Wake Forest. It was a complete culture shock, with a similar sex and dating culture to what I'd known in my hometown. And yet, by that point, I was in a different mental state—I made a promise to myself to focus on football and my grades, so I wasn't as much of a party boy. I think if I had gone right from my high school to FAU, I would be on a completely different path, and not a better one.

During my first season at FAU, I went home to Jupiter during a break, where I met a girl, Mariah. One of my teammates introduced us. She was a freshman at Florida State. As it turned out, we grew up right around the corner from each other—she went to one of the rival high schools and lived only a few streets away. We had so much in common, it was weird that we'd never crossed paths. We hit it off immediately.

I suppose it's worth mentioning that, at the time, I still didn't think I wanted to be in a relationship. Even though I'd stopped the all-out partying, I was the new kid at school and on the team, and I wanted to get the lay of the land before I made any big commitments. That included girls. I was at the top of my game when it came to both football and school, and I didn't want to get distracted. And I was still, on some deep level, afraid of being hurt. And yet, I couldn't help falling for Mariah. All the pieces were there. I was so attracted to her, I loved her personality, I loved her energy. From the time I met her, I was head over heels. She is a fun, easygoing person, and everyone who knows her loves her. She was exciting to be around and easy to talk to. Our relationship was the most comfortable dynamic I'd ever been a part of.

On a different level, I also loved what she had going on at home. I came from a broken family, and her parents were happily together. Their whole family—Mariah, her parents, and her two siblings— lived in Florida, right on the water, in what seemed to be (in my eyes) this idyllic existence. Their home, and everything she came from, was my dream. We had the same ideals, and for the first time, it was easy for me to envision a future together with someone. I was like, *That's it, right there.* We had such a good time together; I wanted more and more and more, which was a feeling I'd never had before. I wanted to hold her hand—let me tell you, I hadn't wanted to hold a girl's hand since my first heartbreak. I wanted to snuggle her, which was also new for me.

Our relationship took off. We spent our whole winter break together back home in Jupiter. After two incredible weeks, she went back to FSU and I went back to FAU, but we stayed together, and I slipped back into my old lovey-dovey self. I sent her flowers. I sent her all these mushy, romantic texts. It was a whole new world for me. I hadn't behaved this way since I was back in middle school. My boys were all like, "What's gotten into you?" They even told Mariah, "I've never seen him act this way before." Mariah's birthday was in January, and I went up to FSU to see her. I remember spending Super Bowl Sunday together, going to these parties and events as a couple. No matter where we went or who we were with, we always had a great time together. As the year went on, I became completely infatuated with her.

That summer, Mariah was supposed to have an internship in Tallahassee, but when the time came, she decided to spend the summer in Jupiter with me. One afternoon, we were out on the boat together, and she told me, "I think I L-O-V-E you." I'd never said that to anyone before, but once the words were out there, I didn't even hesitate. I immediately told her, "I love you, too." That was one of the most amazing feelings I've known.

We went on to have the most incredible summer ever. We went to St. Petersburg and traveled all around Florida together. I spent a lot of time with her mom, dad, and siblings—her parents made dinner, and we all hung out together, one big happy family. It was everything I'd ever dreamed of. It was honestly the best summer of my life.

As fall approached, football season came back around. Mariah surprised me at my first game, where she saw me score my first-ever college touchdown. As an athlete, that's a dream come true, and to have your support system there to witness it, that was an incredible feeling.

Throughout our relationship, Mariah was always there for me. She was super supportive through all my ups and downs. She poured herself into the relationship, and I started to take that support for granted. This was my first real relationship, and I didn't know any better. I hadn't learned yet that healthy relationships are two-way streets.

When football season was over, it was time to start training for the NFL. It was an insane amount of work, and I was busy all the time. As always, Mariah was there to support me. She came to stay with me in Fort Lauderdale, where I was training. I had a condo to myself, and we played house and were all lovey-dovey. Even though I was working so hard, life was frickin' amazing during that time, and I was starting to envision my whole future with Mariah. Marriage, kids, everything.

Then the NFL draft came. I didn't get picked up, even after all my hard work. I was crushed. But then I got a call a few days later that the Baltimore Ravens were picking me up, and in a moment, it felt like I had been saved.

That's the day my relationship went sideways.

That night, my buddies and I—essentially, everyone who got drafted or picked up—planned to go out and celebrate. We were out at a bar, having fun, when a beautiful girl walked by us and caught everyone's attention. She quickly became the topic of conversation, as my buddies made it clear they wanted to invite her to join us all on my boat the following day. The only catch was that no one had the courage to go talk to her. Meanwhile, I was clearly feeling confident, even cocky, now that I had been drafted. So I took it upon myself to go and talk to her for the group.

I approached her, I got her number, and I invited her to join us on the boat the next day. To be clear, I only talked to her on behalf of my buddies. I had no intention of anything happening, with this girl or with anyone else. I would never have cheated on Mariah, that's just not me, and I've never cheated in a relationship. But I still joked around with my friends, saying things like, "I still got game even though I'm wifed up!" That was as far as it went.

But I know now that when it came to Mariah's comfort level, that was taking it a step too far. Later on, Mariah saw me talking to that girl on my boat, and she decided to investigate. And honestly? She should be in the FBI. I think we all know a girl like that, someone super observant who can sleuth together a case via social media with very little evidence. In this case, it took Mariah a split second to know something was up. She logged in to my Instagram account from her own phone and went through my messages. She saw the jokes I'd been saying to my friends, including how I still had game.

Though there was nothing at all going on with the girl, no messages between us for Mariah to see, she was still upset by what she read. In that way, I take full responsibility for crossing a line of trust and making Mariah feel uncomfortable. However, I should also say that going through someone's account is never the right thing to do. Trust is something you have to build together.

That was our first real hiccup. Looking back at it, I was wrong, and I understand why she felt betrayed. Even though I didn't cheat, I made Mariah feel like I was interested in another girl, which led to feelings of insecurity. What's more, my actions, particularly the way I talked to my buddies, were disrespectful to her. I shouldn't have said those things. But at the time, I saw no harm in doing so, and I couldn't see what reason she had to be upset. I was seeing our relationship in black and white and couldn't accept that I had done something wrong in the gray area. I wasn't empathetic to her feelings at all. That situation created a lot of insecurities for her, and it led our relationship to a rocky place.

My buddies and I had an ongoing group chat where we talked about all sorts of things, including some of the girls we went to school with. After that first fight, Mariah would look through my phone and read everything we said. It led to us bickering all the time. Both of us felt betrayed—I felt like she was overstepping her boundaries by keeping watch over my accounts, but she felt like she couldn't trust me and that she had no other choice.

While all this was happening, I suffered a disappointment of my own: I got cut from the Ravens minicamp. My dreams were crushed. This whole cycle happened twice—I got a call, I got my hopes up, and then I got cut. The second time it happened, I fell into a deep depression. It got so bad, I didn't want to leave my room. I stayed in bed, watching show after show. I didn't want to do anything. I didn't want to be seen in public. I couldn't bring myself to face the world. I especially didn't want Mariah's parents to see me, because I thought they would think I was a failure. I just wanted to be alone and feel hurt. But anyone who's experienced depression will understand what a slippery slope that can be. The more I isolated, the more I dug myself deeper and deeper into that hole.

As always, Mariah was there for me. She tried her best to help me, pushing me to go work out and attempting to get me out of the house. She suggested things for us to do together. She invited me to spend time with her family. But I couldn't bring myself to do any of it. "They don't want a failure around," I told her, choosing to stay home instead. To me, the world only got uglier as time went on. I felt like I couldn't do anything right. When my parents hit hard times, they turned away from their relationship instead of leaning into it. Looking back, I realize that I was falling into that exact same pattern.

While I was trying to cope with my situation, Mariah was in a tough place of her own. She had a lot of uncertainty around her future; she was getting ready to graduate and couldn't figure out what she wanted to do career-wise. I see now that I didn't help her with that. I didn't offer up the support she needed. I was so wrapped up in my own dreams falling apart that I couldn't see that she needed me to be there for her, too.

Eventually, my dad was able to convince me to start training again. For six months, my life became all about work and working out. Every day, I got up at 5:00 a.m. and trained for two hours, then worked construction all day, and then trained for another two hours at night. It was miserable. I was miserable. But eventually, the Spring League accepted me into their developmental program, so it seemed my hard work had paid off.

During this time, my relationship with Mariah turned ugly. She still didn't trust me, and we argued constantly. I didn't know how to make it better. I was afraid to break up with her. I recognized that it wasn't working, but I was scared to be alone. I didn't confront our issues head-on or do anything to reassure her. I couldn't make the decision to let her go. Instead, I did one of the worst things you can do in a relationship—I just let it drag on, even when it became clear that breaking up would be the best thing for both of us.

Mariah tried her best to keep the relationship going. She would drive seven hours to come cheer me up, she would check in to make sure I was doing all right, but I took it all for granted. She poured all of herself into keeping the relationship alive, and then, when she needed me, I only gave a half-ass effort to return that love.

I never cheated, but I wasn't giving her the respect she deserved or being protective of her emotions. I would look at other girls on social media and imagine how the grass would be greener in another relationship. I've since come to understand that Instagram is a world of instant gratification, where the grass *always* looks greener somewhere else. What I eventually learned is that some other grass may look greener, but in reality, the grass is greenest wherever you water it.

It's up to you. If you pour yourself into your relationship and you work together to make it stronger, that's the best thing there is. That was a big lesson for me, and one that was hard to learn. I carry it with me to this day and know better than to take something good for granted again.

But twenty-six-year-old me had a lot to learn. With Mariah, things were in a rocky place. Then one day, during Spring League, Mariah looked through my phone again and saw that some girl had sent me a nude. I didn't know this person, and it wasn't solicited. We had never even spoken before! I had a bit of a profile due to my budding football career. This may sound a bit crass, but it's not entirely uncommon to receive unsolicited explicit messages once that happens. The best you can do is block the account or number when it happens. But Mariah and I were already running low on trust. When she saw that message, she (understandably) got upset. It crushed her. That was the straw that broke the camel's back. From where I stand today, I can see that the right thing (and certainly the most faithful thing) to do would have been to block the girl as soon as she sent the nude. But I didn't, which allowed her to keep sending. It was just a couple days later, while I was on the road with my dad, that Mariah called and broke up with me.

And that was that.

I regretted everything immediately. But by that point, there was nothing I could do to fix it, nothing I could do to convince her otherwise. Most important, there was nothing I could do to go back and prevent myself from hurting her in the first place. I had my chance with a girl I loved, and I blew it.

After the road trip, I got back to town and asked, "Can I take you out for breakfast?" She agreed.

We met up one morning, and I saw firsthand how hurt she was. We sat at the Berry Fresh Cafe and talked about everything—all the shit I did, what I put her through, how we both felt about the breakup. That was pretty hard for me. It was heartbreaking to see the role I played in bringing about the end of our relationship, not to mention the pain I had caused her. But it was also a wake-up call. Even though there was no way to repair my relationship with Mariah, from that point forward, I promised myself I would never do that to somebody ever again. Our past mistakes don't have to define our future relationships, and through that experience, I learned that it's possible to grow.

What I know now is that relationships are all about maintaining a balance, especially when it comes to give and take. You and your partner have to both give and take at different times, in different ways, depending on what's going on in each of your lives. Some days you'll need all your partner's support, and some days they'll need all of yours. Most days it won't be that extreme. But the important thing is that both people feel heard and respected and supported. You can take that support when you need it, but you must also be ready to offer it back.

In my relationship with Mariah, I came to see that all I did was take. She poured so much of herself into the relationship—driving hours to watch my games, giving me emotional support, trying to lift my spirits when I was down. She put so much value into me, and I never learned how to offer her that value in return. I couldn't help but think if I had done the best I could, if I'd given her the same kind of support that she'd shown me, our relationship would've gone differently. It would've been a whole other story. Instead, I had to fuck up and learn the hard way. But sometimes, that's the way life goes.

The truth is, at that time, we both had a lot of learning and growing to do individually. Even if Mariah had said something to make me realize how I was behaving, I think I still would have needed the time and space to figure it out on my own. Every time she explained how she felt or gave me a chance to do better, I would say and do all the right things at first, only to mess everything up again. I learned that sometimes, when a situation is toxic, the best thing to do is to cut your losses. Our issues weren't because of who Mariah was, or even about our compatibility, but because of my own internal conflicts at that stage in my life. I was miserable and lonely, not to mention still figuring out who I was and who I wanted to be. It sent me looking for attention in the wrong places.

After some reflection, I saw that in order to be good—a good person, a good partner—I needed to take accountability for my actions. So, step by step, I started taking accountability for everything. I poured all of myself into the last of my classes, into studying to get my MBA. I poured everything into getting my general contractor's license. I showed up, and I worked, and I studied. I realized: *It's my money, and it's my time. I have to be accountable.*

While I'm admitting all the ways I screwed up in my first real relationship, I'll tell you something else I'm not proud of. In order to finish my MBA, I had to take three summer classes: Finance II, Accounting II, and a final business class. I was scared to take them, because when I took Finance I and Accounting I as an undergrad, I cheated my way through them. The classes weren't proctored, and I completely took advantage; I sat there and used Google to find the answers. When the level II classes came, I was like, *Oh shit.* Not only could I not cheat my way through them again (not that I would have wanted to at that point), but I didn't have the knowledge of the classes that came before them. It may sound cliché, but it's true that the only person I'd cheated was myself. I had no choice but to sit down and learn all the things I hadn't learned the first time around.

I treated it like a job. I spent seven hours a day learning all I could. I locked in and studied my ass off. At first, I had no idea what I was doing. But just like I would during the hike at Zion, I started at the bottom and put one foot in front of the other. At the end of the summer, I got better grades in those two classes than I did in the classes where I had cheated.

Once I put the work in, I saw that I could actually get A's on my own. I was capable of figuring things out if I just put in the effort. People had written excuses for me my whole life. Since I had been a jock, all that mattered was that I succeeded on the field. My teachers, parents, and even my peers didn't really expect me to excel academically, so I set low expectations for myself, too. Taking responsibility for my actions was a much better way to do things. It gave me another notch of confidence. It felt better, for so many reasons. That was another big lesson for me.

After getting my MBA, I decided to go a step further and get my general contractor's license. Before I started, my dad told me, "That's the hardest test you can take in Florida." At the very first class I attended, one of the other students went home crying. There were terms I had never heard before; I had no idea what was going on. I felt screwed. But I paid $3,000 for the class, and that was what I wanted, so I committed to making it work. I got the books and put one foot in front of the other, just hammering it out. After a month of working hard, I took the test. I got a ninety-two, an eighty-seven, and an eighty-six on the exam sections, which were some of the highest scores in the class. The guy who was proctoring the test told me, "I've never seen someone score this high on their first try."

Now, a couple things were at play here. The first was that I started to believe in myself. The second was that just like I would on that hike, I put my head down and started working, piece by piece, trusting that if I just put one foot in front of the other, good things would come. Following that approach, I was able to get my master's degree, which no one else in my family had ever done, as well as my general contractor's license. And best of all, I did it on my own. As life started to come together, I finally had confidence in myself, and confidence will take you far.

Once I started really showing up for my own life, I saw that every action has a reaction. With every situation you approach, a good or a bad thing can come from it, and a lot of times the difference is up to you. And then, even so-called bad outcomes can be transformed into positives if you take accountability and learn from them.

What does this have to do with relationships? First, you have to take accountability for yourself. Then you need to bring that same confidence and accountability you build to the rest of your life and apply that to your relationships. It's like that old saying, that you need to love yourself before you can love another. Before you can show up in a relationship, you need to show up for yourself.

We all have our fears, our distractions, our vices. There's a side of me that still feels like I want to focus on fun more than anything else. I want to drink and party and hang out with my friends. But I think that being ready for a relationship is knowing how to balance your needs with your partner's. I also think a lot of it has to do with maturity. I saw that being the man I wanted to be in a relationship started by being a good guy in all areas of my life. If you want something better, you need to take the actions that will lead to the life you want.

After reflecting on everything I learned from Mariah, I stopped being a finger pointer and started being a thumb pointer. Let me explain. There are people who, when something goes wrong, immediately start pointing their finger at everyone else. *Whose fault is it? Who can I blame?* But that's not how you learn and grow. Instead, you need to point the thumb back at yourself, to own up to your mistakes and accept the blame that belongs to you. Every relationship involves two people, and both of them play a role in building it up or breaking it down. We're all going to fuck up occasionally, but if we take accountability for our mistakes, we can grow and get past them. (And if we don't, then get ready, because it's going to be the same circle of bullshit over and over again.)

That's why, when I was on *The Bachelorette*, I always defended Hannah. I saw some of the other guys on the show taking from Hannah but not giving back in return. I offered her support however I could. I defended her choices, and I defended her to the other guys whenever anyone said shit about her behind her back. I knew how I had treated my ex—she poured so much value into our relationship but didn't get any of it back—and I didn't ever want that to happen to Hannah.

These days, I look at my romantic relationships the same way I look at my relationships with my best friends. I stick up for them. I take care of them. I make sure they're okay. At the end of the day, your boyfriend, girlfriend, or spouse isn't just your partner; they're also your best friend. Sometimes, people create drama and problems in relationships just to get over them, or "test" the other person to see where they stand. But if you look at your relationships with your closest friends, you would never do that. If you wouldn't say or do something to your friends, why would you do that to someone you have romantic feelings for? In an ideal relationship, you want to always act from a place of trust and loyalty.

The way I see it, if you're committing yourself to someone, you owe them all of you. You owe them the best of you. Even if your worst side comes out on occasion (we all have our moments), you owe it to them to find a way to circle back to your best self.

When it comes to a partner, I want someone who is accountable. I want to be with a person who, when shit doesn't go their way, doesn't automatically blame others but also examines themselves. I'm looking for someone who has so much belief and confidence in herself and someone who wants to be a boss, meaning she wants to take charge of her goals, dreams, and ambitions. It doesn't matter what she wants to do—it could be anything—just that she wants to go make it happen. I want us to motivate each other. I want to be able to cheer her on, and I want her to be able to cheer me on. I want that balance of give and take.

Because in the end, a relationship is comprised of two individual people, and each one needs to have their own dreams, goals, and aspirations. It's okay to have some shared ones, too, and you should always be supportive of what your partner wants to achieve. But while you're still growing, you need to make decisions that let you become your best self. Your own goals need to be the most important, and you shouldn't sacrifice your dreams for another person. Your perfect person won't ever ask you to. There might be compromise, and once you start a family, shared plans and dreams might replace individual ones. But if each of you is living your best life, being who you are and going after what you want, then the relationship has the space to be its own thing—a partnership that enhances both your lives.

My past relationships definitely weren't perfect, but I'm so thankful for them. They inspired a journey of work and reflection, and they helped me become the person I am today. Every relationship, even the ones that end in disaster, has something good to teach us. When a relationship doesn't work out, the best things you can do are to reflect, grow, and learn, so you don't make the same mistakes twice.

Figure your shit out so you don't repeat your patterns. If you do that, you'll be all the better for it. And one day, you'll feel ready to take that step toward the right thing.

The Real Tyler:

· ·

ACCORDING TO HIS FRIEND MOLLIE

One of my most notorious Tyler stories happened when we were freshmen in high school. Back then, I used to tutor Tyler. He would probably like to say that we "did our homework together," but it was definitely a one-way street. One day after school, he was at my place, sitting at the kitchen table. My mom went to pick up my brother from soccer practice, leaving Tyler and me alone. He stayed for another twenty minutes or so, until it got dark, and then he left. I kept sitting at the table doing my work.

Ten minutes later, I heard the front door open and slam shut. My back was to the door, so I whipped around but didn't see anyone there.

"Hello?" I said.

There was no response.

I said my brother's name, but no one answered.

I called my mom and asked, "Are you home?" She told me she was still in the parking lot waiting for my brother.

Now I was panicking.

Suddenly, a gigantic figure in a black hoodie, with the hood turned around so it covered their face, came running at me. I was convinced that was the end.

Then, the gigantic figure wrapped me in a hug. I saw his shoes and instantly realized who it was. I collapsed to the floor, hysterically sobbing, when Tyler said, "That's to teach you to lock your doors when you're home alone!"

We have an almost sibling-like relationship. There is no fear with anything he says or does. He makes jokes and pulls pranks, and sometimes they terrorize me, but he thinks they're funny.

When I think of Tyler, I think of Troy Bolton, the protagonist from *High School Musical*, because Tyler so desperately wanted to be him. He knew all the dance moves and all the words to every *High School Musical* number. For probably four years after those movies came out, Tyler would spontaneously break out in song. It's funny, because he's a relatively good dancer, so that part he can pull off. But he's one of the worst singers I've ever heard, and he's always belting out every song that pops into his head.

When it came to his early romantic relationships, I think he also wanted to be Troy Bolton. He's super romantic and also a very affectionate person. If he could sit and have someone playing with his hair or rubbing his back all day long, he would be down for that. I think his love language is definitely touch; he's a very present, lovey person. He loves love, and he tries to love on everyone.

I've had multiple boyfriends while I've been friends with Tyler, and I think any normal, rational guy would be intimated by his being my best friend, but in reality, I've never encountered that. It's a testament to how Tyler handles things and how he's able to make people super comfortable. Now, my boyfriend and Tyler are really close. Ty always makes a point to include him and has gone out of his way to be welcoming to him, because it's clear to both of them that the other is around to stay. People who know him just don't hate him; it doesn't happen.

I think it's special when Tyler calls me, because he genuinely wants to know my opinion. You know how sometimes a friend will ask you things but they don't really listen? Or they'll ask for your advice but not take it? Tyler is the opposite of that. If he's running something by me, I know it's because he truly wants to know what I think.

When he hangs out with you, he really wants to talk things through. It's not chitchat or gossip, but when it comes to making decisions, he wants to dissect them. That often comes along with a glass of wine and a face mask. Tyler is always down for a good face mask. Also, from the time I've known him, since he was around five ten up until the height he is now, he loves baths. It might be the funniest thing ever, to see this giant man in a bathtub, soaking with music and a candle. He loves pampering himself.

When you're with Tyler, you're always going to have a good time. He's never going to let it be boring. He's a great storyteller, and he'll bring up these stories full of details I would never have remembered. I think the reason his memory is so good is because he truly values his experiences and wants to hold on to them.

When Tyler told me he was going to be on *The Bachelorette*, I actually hadn't watched it before, so I didn't understand that in the end, people hope to come out engaged. I didn't grasp the stakes; my reaction was just, "I can't wait to see you on TV. You're going to say the dumbest shit. This is going to be so entertaining!" But I do think he had a life-changing experience on the show. He thinks it's one of the best decisions he's ever made. Even though he got his heart broken—which I hadn't known upon his return—he said it was such a good experience. It was almost like someone talking about having an awakening. I expected his account to be all drama, all the time, but instead it was a transformative experience. He really took it as an opportunity to reflect on who he is as a person.

I would never have thought of Tyler as a "feminist icon," but once that was out there, it all adds up. Tyler grew up with a mom who was super strong—she was the head of the house, she made all the rules, and she didn't take any bullshit. (She had to be that way; she was dealing with three very headstrong boys' boys.) I think he saw her as his first role model. Now, he has so many friends who are girls, and he respects every woman he encounters. I think he truly does believe that he's nothing without the women in his life. He almost takes it to an extreme, where he thinks we have all the answers—which I'll take!

Tyler is such a people person. He's one of those people who knows everyone everywhere he goes. Even when he doesn't know them, you'd think that he does. He'll have a long conversation with the server and you'd think they're best friends. Every year, he got my school schedule switched so we could be in math class together. That wasn't common—the school wouldn't let anyone switch their schedule; you were stuck with what you got—but he got close with the guidance counselor. A part of me always figured he would be successful and well-known.

Still, the way it happened overnight was shocking. One week, everything was normal; and then one day, while the show was still airing, we went to a bar together, and he got swarmed. My jaw dropped; I had no idea what was going on. Over time, I got used to it, but it's funny because I still see him as Tyler; and he still is. People will ask me about him, and they'll be freaking out, and I'm like, "Guys, it's Tyler. The goofy hometown quarterback with the biggest heart."

When I see him on TV, doing interviews, he's 100 percent himself. People ask me all the time if what you see on TV is who he really is, and the answer is yes. That's not a persona. He was made for this. I don't know how he does it, but I think it comes naturally to him. Tyler is someone who is very comfortable in his skin.

3

. . . .

MY FIRST LOVE

. . . .

What I Learned from Playing Sports

It's safe to say my first true love was sports. I was born on January 31, which fell on Super Bowl Sunday. Right after I was born, they put me in the bassinet next to a *Florida Sportsman* magazine and a Florida Gators football. That's what made it into all my baby pictures—a fishing magazine and a ball. That kind of tells you everything you need to know, both about what a redneck my dad is and also about where my life was headed. Sports and the outdoors have pretty much been my life.

Growing up, I always heard my dad talk about playing football—it's part of what bonded the two of us so much. When he was younger, he played college football and tried going pro. Ever since I was a little kid, he always had that blueprint for success that he had followed, and he instilled a love of hard work into me. My dad was that crazy sports dad (you know the one). He came to every practice and every game, and he always pushed me to give it all I had. He likes to tell this story about my very first football game, in seventh grade. I was running down the field when a kid put his helmet in my shin. It hurt like hell and I started crying, so my dad came over to see what the deal was. I asked him if I was okay to play.

"Can you stand?" he asked.

I stood.

"Can you walk?"

I walked.

"Can you run?"

I ran.

"You're good to play," he said. "Get going."

So I went back out there and I played. Not only that, but I played like I was out to destroy the other team. That was when he realized he had a beast on his hands. That was the kind of tough love that I was used to receiving from my dad. As a kid, it was the only thing I knew.

In high school, I earned the nickname Bam-Bam, because I was a bruiser. I was a six-three center on the basketball team, going up against players who were six seven and six eight, so I was really physical because I knew that was how I could compensate for my size. My first thirty seconds of my varsity basketball career wound up leading to a six-week suspension for starting a brawl. There was a girl in my class, Jenna, who would always make fun of me because I was a typical jock. "My name is Tyler," she would say, in this stereotypical jock voice, "and football is my favorite vegetable." Football determined my friends and how people saw me around school. It also defined how I saw myself.

In our town growing up, baseball was prominent—everyone played it, and there were a lot of politics involved. We called it "daddy ball," because it was the kind of thing where your dad had to be the coach in order for you to play. But when it came to football, I was just so good that there was no question of whether I deserved to be on the field. The first two times I ever touched the ball, I scored.

My dad gave me pointers, but more than anything, he taught me how important a work ethic is. If you want to be the best, you have to practice harder than everyone else. Throughout my basketball career, there is one day that sticks out. When I was in fifth grade, we were at a tournament in another part of Florida, and during the first game, I was playing soft. My job was to box out the other team, and I wasn't doing it very well at all. My dad was not amused. I remember him telling me, "I didn't drive all this way to watch you stand around and watch the ball." More of his typical hard-nosing.

After the game, the whole team left to go to dinner before the second game later that night. As everyone's cars went down the road, one by one, they all turned left. My dad turned right.

"Where are we going?" I asked.

"We're going to go work some more," he said.

While everyone else ate dinner, my dad and I went to an empty parking lot, where he made me put my back against his truck and push it around the lot. (I was a pretty big kid.) I did that for two hours, until it was time for the next game. As crazy as his method might seem, it worked. With the next team, I was a boxing-out machine. No one could get by me. My dad taught me that I may not always be the biggest, the strongest, or the fastest, but I can always be the hardest-working person out there.

If high school football practice started at 9:00 a.m., my dad would drive me and my buddy down to the field at 7:30 or 8:00. We would jump the six-foot chain-link fence and put in an hour of work before practice even started. Later in the day, he would take me to this place called the Pit, which was basically an area with hills—the only hills in South Florida—made out of sugar sand, which is this super-soft sand that you sink into. I don't know how the hell he found it, but that became our place. We would go there all the time and work. We ran up the hills, up and down, up and down, often when the sun was right overhead, during the hottest part of the day. It made me a good runner when it came to playing football, and it taught me to be grittier and stronger when the going got tough.

At the very top of the hill, I'd encounter what my dad called "rare air," that air not many people work hard enough to get to breathe. Not many people made it up there to the tops of the dunes; not that many people were willing to do the huffing and puffing that was necessary to get there. He taught me that rare air extends beyond those hills—no matter where you are, at the top of any big challenge, you'll often find that not many people are willing to put in that kind of hard work. The goal is to breathe as much rare air as possible.

He also taught me that if you work really hard at something, you won't be surprised when you get an accolade or an award because you'll know that you've earned it. If you've given it your all, and you know you've outworked the people around you, you approach opportunities knowing that you belong and that you deserve them. The pride and confidence that goes with that knowledge are very good feelings.

My dad introduced me to the side of myself that is a hard-nosed grinder. Nothing can stop me. I was the guy who ran people over. My shoulder would pop out, and I'd pop it back in and keep on playing. Whenever we worked out together, my dad said the one thing that scared him about me was that I set no limits for myself. I never took breaks, and I never stopped. No matter how hard anyone pushed me, I'd always keep going. As my dad would say, "You're all gas and no brakes." He always said I had no speed limit when it came to hard work.

The result was that I outworked everybody and got my first college offer when I was just a freshman in high school. This taught me a lesson that is true for all of us, no matter what you do. In sports and in life, you get out of it what you put in. If you work at something, you will see results. I promise. If you haven't seen the result you want yet, then you haven't put in enough work to get there. It's that simple. A lot of people want this or that, and a lot of people have talent, but unless you put that work in, you're never going to achieve it.

One of my dad's favorite pieces of advice—he has a lot of them—was "Quit settling for what's good right now. Put the hard work in so you can have a bigger payout later." This applies not only to sports but also to any goal you're after in life. You can cash in wherever you're at, or you can keep your eye on the prize. Instant gratification feels good in that moment, but not as good as you'll feel after you've put in the effort to accomplish what you *really* want.

Through sports, perhaps more than anything else, there were so many little things I learned along the way. I had a football coach at Wake Forest—if I'm being honest, we couldn't stand each other—who had a thing called Deacon Time. In essence, he started everything, from meetings to practices, ten minutes early. If practice was called for 10:00 a.m., it was actually going to start at 9:50, Deacon Time. I think that's why, to this day, I've never been late for a meeting. If I schedule something, I'll never miss it or cancel last minute or even show up a few minutes late. Punctuality is huge to me. I learned it from a football coach, but it also matters a lot in the business world.

Sports taught me resilience. Outside of the hard work I needed to put in, my time as a football player was full of other challenges. When I first arrived at college at Wake Forest, I redshirted my first year. (That's when you essentially spend the year doing practice but not playing in actual games. It gives you time to improve as a player and extends the amount of time you're eligible to play college football.) It felt frustrating to sit on the bench all year, even though I was training so hard. But then at the end of my freshman year, my coach was like, "Tyler, this is your team now. It's time for you to take over." That was my dream, and I was ready. It was time to lock it in.

Then two weeks later, that head coach got fired. A new coach came in, along with a whole new staff. All the credibility I had built with my old coach no longer mattered, and I had to start earning the respect of the new staff from scratch. I didn't have any choice but to try to appease them, so I did everything the coach said to get in his good graces. He wanted me to get strong, so I became one of the strongest guys on the team. I went from being a 200-pound kid to a real meathead at 225 pounds. I tried to kiss his ass, because playing college football was my dream. I just wanted to win the job as the quarterback.

On the first day of summer, all the new freshmen came in for the start of training. Before this point, in the quarterback room, my chair was all the way in front, like the top dog. But when the new kids came in, the coach moved my chair to the back of the quarterback room. The guys who were the top quarterbacks were seated closest to the TV, while the backups were relegated to the back of the room. By all accounts, this was a bad sign. I remember calling my dad and saying, "No matter how good I play, there's no shot I'm going to be quarterback. These people don't fuck with me at all."

I played the best football of my life that summer. But it didn't matter. I had to battle it out with a new quarterback, Bub, a freshman who was one of the new coach's recruits. I remember having the most perfect scrimmage you could have—I was nine for nine for 250 yards—and they still named Bub as the starter.

That was gut-wrenching, and I was hurt. But looking back, I can see that I played a role in this dynamic, too. To be completely fair, I was playing well, but I wasn't the perfect teammate. I was still partying a lot and not devoting all my time to the team the way I could have.

One way after another, the new coach tried to drive me out of the program.

Midway through the season, our quarterback got hurt, and it was my opportunity to play. On the third play, I tore my MCL and my meniscus in my left knee, but I knew that I couldn't take time off, in order to show other schools my ability.

The next day during practice I could barely walk. The coach told me to go to the training room, saying there was no need to join the team meetings. This continued all week. He kept sending me to the training room—I never went to a single meeting.

During every practice throughout that week, the coaches would make me go to the trainers, and the trainers would make me roll the entire time. In the football world, rolling is torture. It's a form of punishment coaches use in college football, to make someone dizzy and sick. It usually happens when a player is late to something, a meeting or a practice, to try to teach them a lesson. Essentially, the way it works is that you do a sit-up, then you roll over and do a push-up, then you roll onto your back and do a sit-up, then a push-up, and you just keep on doing that until someone tells you to stop. My knee was injured, and every time I rolled over to do a push-up, it would bang on the ground, making the whole thing nearly unbearable. I told them over and over how much it was hurting me, but the trainers didn't care.

After a week of rolling, I was notified that I was traveling to our next game. I was dumbfounded by this news, since I hadn't been permitted to go to one practice. When game day came around, the offensive coordinator said, in front of everybody, "Tyler, we don't need you." That caught me off guard. All my teammates kept asking me what was going on, and I said I had no idea, only that the coaches had been weird all week. The whole team was getting dressed for the game, and I asked the trainer, "What am I supposed to do?" I hadn't practiced all week. He told me to ask the QB coach. "Am I supposed to dress up?" I asked him, to which he replied, "Do what you want." So I didn't.

We lost the game to Boston College. But I was about to lose a lot more. The next morning, I got a text from the head coach to meet him in his office. I thought that meant I was finally going to get some clarity about what the heck was going on.

When I arrived, I saw that my strength coach was there, the head of compliance was there . . . something was definitely up. *Oh shit*, I thought, *it's about to go down.* I was right. The head coach basically told me, "I think it's best we go our separate directions."

I was devastated.

This was the last thing I wanted. I'm the kind of person who, when I start something, I want to finish it. I told him I wanted to stay, but he said that wasn't possible.

I asked him if I could be the scout team quarterback, and he said no.

"If you don't want me to play anymore, can I help out in any way?" I asked.

"No," he said. "We don't want you here."

He told me I would never play there again. That was it. That was all he said. He never even gave me a reason.

What made it even nastier was the part that came next. "I have to tell the media why you're not on the team anymore," he said. Then he gave me an ultimatum. I could either say I was cut from the team because of disciplinary actions, or I could say it was because I injured my shoulder and I needed time to rehab it.

Now, neither one of these options was true, and neither one was good. He needed to offer some explanation to the outside world as to why he was cutting me, and he was willing to trash my name in order to save his own. The truth is, I think that from the very beginning, he labeled me as a party boy and never gave me a fair shot as a player. While there is some truth to that assessment—because I did spend a lot of time partying—I think I could have been both. But I never got the chance to prove myself.

If I couldn't play at Wake Forest, I was going to try to play somewhere else. I didn't want anyone from any other school to think I was damaged goods. But I definitely didn't want to take the fall for disciplinary actions—or even just a report of disciplinary actions—for things I hadn't done and be labeled a troublemaker. Because I had no other choice, I told him to say that I hurt my shoulder.

I was so upset that I went home and cried. That was a real rejection, the worst I'd ever known. Not only did the new coach not see my potential, he didn't even give me a shot to prove my abilities to him.

Before this happened, I lived on a hall with ten other guys from the team. As soon as I was cut from the team, I moved out and was alone. One thing I realized while going through that experience was that I have a real fear of being by myself; I hated it at first. But being alone had an upside, too, in that it gave me the time and space to reflect. I asked myself, how did I get to this point? What events led up to this happening? What could I have done differently that might have made this go in another direction?

When I looked back at what happened at Wake Forest, I could see that yes, my coaches definitely mishandled it. But I didn't do the best job, either. I looked at my roommate, another football player I lived with my freshman year, who remained on the team and played the entire time he was at school. How did he do that? Why was he in the position he was in? I saw that he was disciplined, and he worked hard. He never partied the way that I had. I always tiptoed the line between good and bad, while he remained squarely on the good side. He was responsible. He was always the one who drove me home after a night out.

On paper, I was a more talented player than this guy. I was bigger, stronger, faster. So why was he in his position, and I was in mine? I could see the answer was because he kept on working—he put one foot in front of the other. I let partying and being out and about consume too much of my time and energy. And while I was at it, I wasn't always the best football player, teammate, friend. Did I agree with my coach's decision? Of course not. But could I also have done a better job to stay on the team? Yes.

After I took some time to reflect on what happened, I told myself, *If I ever get the chance to play football at another school, I'm going to be like my roommate.* But it wasn't going to be that simple. At first, no one wanted to take me. Everyone thought I had shoulder problems because that was what was reported in the news. But eventually, two schools came calling. The first was Wagner College, on Staten Island, New York, which has a small football program. They offered me a full scholarship, which was hard to pass up. The second was Florida Atlantic University, which offered me a walk-on position. I signed my papers to go to Wagner, because I didn't want my parents to have to pay for my mistakes. A few weeks later, FAU called and told me a scholarship had opened up. What was more, they asked me if I wanted to play quarterback.

After sitting on the boat and talking it through with my dad— weighing the options of, in his words, "freezing in New York versus playing football in sunny Florida"—I decided to go with FAU. But this time, I was going to get my shit together and do it right. I wouldn't waste another opportunity to do what I loved.

From the moment I arrived, I was up against another quarterback there. He was a senior and the team captain, and he was always going to be the number one guy. But I reminded myself: I'm not just here for myself. I need to assist any way that I can.

One day, I went to the office and told the coach I could help out as a tight end, and he told me he would give me a try. He threw me in a practice, and the first pass that came my way, I dropped. The next day, he threw me in there again, and I dropped it again. I don't know why the coach decided to give me a third opportunity, but he did. On the third try, I caught the ball and ran with it for almost thirty yards. They saw I was a threat with the ball in my hands.

My coaches said, "Let's try this kid at blocking." I didn't know what I was doing, I had been a quarterback all my life, but they told me, "Just cut this guy off." I did what they said. The guy I cut off wound up being a freshman All-American (and is now a starting linebacker for the San Francisco 49ers). I pushed him back, at least eighteen yards, and we got into a fight. My coaches loved it. The whole team loved it. The energy went through the roof. Everyone was like, "Who the fuck is this kid? Now he's blocking a linebacker!" And that's how I became our starting fullback/tight end. I didn't have the experience, but I told myself, *I'm going to be the best damn full-back/tight end I can.* I won New Comer of the Year that season and was part of the leadership council. I was so proud of those achievements and knew I had worked so hard for them. At the end of my first year, my coach told me, "You have a real shot at playing in the NFL." Those were the words I had always wanted to hear.

That next season, I kept taking it seriously. Football became my full-time job. I didn't drink for the whole year, which was something I had never done before. It was my senior year and I was team captain. I was named Student-Athlete of the Year. I was finally doing all the right things, and I was proud of who I was.

That was the first time I saw how coming up against challenges can be a good thing, because you can use them as an opportunity to learn. From one rejection came another opportunity. From one failed direction came a whole new path.

When the Baltimore Ravens brought me in, the summer after my last collegiate football season, I hoped they were going to sign me. Draft day was finally here. I was doubtful that I would actually get drafted, but I thought there was a good chance that I would get picked up. The draft ended, and I sat by my phone, waiting for my agent to call me. Ten minutes turned into thirty minutes turned into an hour, which eventually turned into three hours. I left everyone in the draft room to go be by myself. My agent finally called me and told me the Ravens were bringing me in for rookie minicamp.

As soon as I heard the news, I was elated, because I knew that if I got my foot in the door, that was all I needed to work my way on to the team. The way minicamp works is that you play for a whole weekend and they cut players as you go. The entire time, I kept thinking, *I gotta get through it, I gotta keep going, I gotta make the team.* On the last day, I was the top-performing tight end, and everyone in the room thought I was the guy getting signed. Instead, at the last second, I ended up getting cut. Once again, I came so close and left feeling devastated.

Two weeks later, they brought me back again, along with two other tight ends. I was the best performer there. As a next step, they brought me to their doctors. I should have lied; I should have told them I was fine, that I had zero previous injuries. But I told the truth. Once the doctors saw how bad my shoulders were, they cut me again.

I wanted to quit right then and there. But my dad encouraged me. He said, "You gotta keep training." I was dating Mariah at the time, and she encouraged me, too. For six months, I trained every day. I had to pay for my living and my training, so I worked construction. At the time, my job was to build all the pools for the Hard Rock Hotel in Fort Lauderdale. I got up at 5:00 a.m. every day, worked with my trainer until 7:00 a.m., went to work my job from 8:00 a.m. until 4:00 p.m., and then trained some more from 5:00 to 7:00 p.m. Forget work-life balance—I had no life at all. I wasn't even sure if I wanted to play football anymore. Those were the most miserable six months of my life.

Throughout all this training, I was hoping for a spot to play in the new developmental program called the Spring League. It was three weeks of football, including two games in front of all the scouts in the NFL and Canadian Football League. When spring came around, I got the call that I was in the league. I was trying to play tight end, but when I got there, they moved me to fullback, which is the most physical position on the field. I was just bashing my head against people. *What am I doing?* I wondered. *Is this worth it?* There I was, just bashing my head all day, probably getting concussions and shaking them off. For all the positive lessons I learned, football is far from perfect and comes with its own risks and sacrifices. But I thought, *I've put all this work in. I have to see it through.*

We played our first game in the Spring League, and I did pretty well. Then it was time for the second. My dad flew in to Austin to watch it. On the first play, I was in. I ran at the defensive end as if I was going to block him and faked him and got open into the flat. It was third and two. I caught the ball from Heisman Trophy–winner Johnny Manziel, turned upfield, hit the cornerback, and got the yardage I needed for a first down. As I was still fighting for more, some dude came around and slung me down, and I fell, landing right on my shoulder. I couldn't move it. And just like that, my NFL dreams blinked out.

This was the absolute worst-case scenario. I knew it; my dad knew it.

"Let's drive," said my dad. And the rest is history.

That moment led to my lowest low. However, as I wrote earlier in this book, it also became my greatest transformation.

Some of the biggest lessons I've learned came from sports. Perhaps the single biggest one, the one I carry with me everywhere, is the importance of teamwork. There's nothing better than being part of a team. I love the camaraderie. I love the bus rides. I love the hard-fought wins. But what I love most about team sports is that people rely on you and you rely on them. You can be as strong and talented as anyone, but in order to be successful, you have to understand the tenets of brother- or sisterhood and respect. When you win, you win as a team.

When I arrived at FAU, I was a transfer student and the new kid on the team. There I was, in a room with all these guys who didn't know me, who could've easily said, "Fuck this kid, he's trying to take our spot." But instead, they brought me in and taught me everything about a new program and a new position. They welcomed me in as if I was one of their own, and they became my brothers. We knew we needed one another in order to accomplish a goal that was bigger than us, and we loved that. We cheered for one another, and we're still cheering—one of my old teammates just had a baby, and I couldn't be happier for him.

When I reflect back on it now, I recognize that one of the amazing things about my experience playing football was that it was welcoming to everyone. Everyone was loved and accepted. Your race didn't matter, where you came from didn't matter, your background didn't matter. Our love for one another, and for that common goal, was what mattered. That kind of relationship has no boundaries. That's a lesson I wish everyone could learn.

I love that sports are also a way to make people feel good. You feel good, your teammates feel good, and so do the people watching. It's not just about winning. There are so many positive aspects, from showing up to trying your best to doing things you thought you couldn't do. Sports just have a way of making people better, more confident versions of themselves.

These days, I miss playing sports. I crave it. I still play in a men's basketball league, in both Florida and New York. I need to have that outlet for my competitive nature, and also a place to feel that camaraderie. Even when it comes to my daily workouts, I hate working out by myself. I usually work out with one or two or three other people. We might all be crammed in my little-ass gym in my garage back home in Florida, but we're still getting it. Having that camaraderie and accountability is the best way to attack workouts. We push one another and cheer one another on. Then, when you see someone hit a goal or do something they didn't believe they could do, that's when the magic starts.

When my dad got sick, my first thought was, *We need to make some changes around here.* So I started running with my family. I'd get them to meet me at a trail, and the only rule was that we had to keep at it for an hour. "I don't care if you walk or run," I told them, "but you have to keep moving the entire time." My family needed to get healthy. Those runs helped them turn a corner.

It felt so good that when I moved to New York City, I said, "I want to see how far I can take this." I started doing group runs in Central Park, open to anyone who wanted to join. When I first posted about it, I expected maybe twenty people to show up, but at our very first run we had a couple hundred. I was blown away. We'd mob through the park—everyone from experienced runners to people who'd never run before. There were people decked out in gear, and young women who just left work and ran with their jeans and purses. I loved the camaraderie there, too, and had so much fun talking to the people who showed up. Everyone had so many different stories. There were some who started running for a family member, others who just quit smoking and needed something to keep them going. People were making friends and forming real connections. That was such an incredible experience for me, and I loved sharing my passion for fitness with others.

Even if running isn't your thing, it can still make you feel good. For anyone who has anything negative or nasty going on in their life, my advice to you is: Go to a marathon. Don't go *run* a marathon; just go watch one. A marathon is one of the most heartwarming things you will ever see. You have people cheering for strangers they've never met, yelling for them and hyping them up. You see people struggling and hurting, and others picking them up and rallying for them to keep going. You see so much unconditional love among people who don't know one another. Plus, there are usually some amazing homemade signs. It may even be a happier place than Disney World.

I ran two marathons in 2019 and did everything you're not supposed to do. Leading up to the Chicago Marathon, I was running well and consistently, but then I hurt myself. I stopped running (which is part of any recovery program), but I also started partying (which definitely is not). Then, the week before the marathon, I got a modeling job in Paris. I brought my brother Austin, expecting that we'd have a chill time, but instead we partied every night. The Thursday night before the race, I partied until the cab picked me up to bring me to the airport. I flew back to Chicago, landed Friday night, slapped on a hydration IV for much of Saturday, and ran the marathon on Sunday morning. The whole way through, I. Was. Dying. Do not recommend.

The New York City Marathon, on the other hand, was amazing. New York Road Runners, the organization that coordinates the marathon, insisted I run with security, in case any spectators tried to run out in front of me. I said it was completely unnecessary, but they wouldn't take no for an answer. (They take safety and security very seriously.) When I got to the start of the race, my security person was the coolest guy ever. As it turned out, he worked as a detective for many years, and as we ran through different parts of the city, he would say, "This is where this thing happened," or, "This is where we had this bust." It was an amazing experience. He was also in much better shape than I was, and he kept pushing me and encouraging me the whole way through. Again, if you want to go far, go with someone else.

As I approached the finish line, I started to tear up. The energy and the feeling of that moment—it's just unreal. I crossed the finish line, and my mom was there to greet me. I put my medal on, and she gave me the biggest hug and then started crying. (I wanted to cry, too, but I had to go on TV! So I managed to keep it together.) Both my mom and my dad were there with me in New York that day, and it was an amazing, amazing moment. It's something I'll always cherish.

Accomplishing a physical goal—no matter how big or small— feels incredible. To that end, if you're not currently taking care of yourself, I challenge you to give it one month. Set a simple goal like going on a run or a walk every day. I promise you'll end that month seeing yourself much differently.

That brings me to my final lesson, but it's also an important one. No matter how bad I feel going into a workout, afterward I always feel better, both about myself and about what I can do. Working out helps give you confidence. If you're going out and meeting somebody—for a date, for a job interview, for anything—try putting in a workout beforehand. I've found that it helps you put your best self forward, and I believe that's the key, more than anything, to success. Just try it! I promise it'll be worth it.

The Real Tyler:

ACCORDING TO HIS HIGH SCHOOL GUIDANCE COUNSELOR, MRS. P

When I met Tyler, he was a mess. A true, true mess. It was right after his first semester of ninth grade, and he was acting out. He was never disrespectful—that's just not Tyler—but he talked too much, he didn't do the work, he incited the other kids. Needless to say, the teachers weren't thrilled to have him in their classes.

He was playing football on the freshman team, and right away it was clear that he was a gifted athlete. Tyler needed to maintain a certain GPA to stay on the team, but his report card that first semester was dreadful. (I think even his phys-ed grade was a D!) My husband, who coached the older kids, brought him to me and said, "This kid's got great potential, but he's screwing up in the classroom. See what you can do."

So we started working together. I remember having a conversation with him about first impressions, when I told him you only get one chance to make one. "Your teachers already think you're a screwup," I explained. "So now you need to prove yourself, and it might take some time." We set about making changes in order to get his teachers to believe in him. "The teacher's favorite may be the kid who does things right from the start," I told him, "but their *second* favorite is the one who decides to turn it all around." And that's exactly what he did.

Over the next three and a half years, Tyler spent an inordinate amount of time in my office. He needed someone who wasn't going to go easy on him, but also someone who he knew was truly in his corner. Our relationship was different from the one he had with his football coach or his teachers, because with me, he could be completely himself, all the time.

When it came to dating, Tyler was always a sweetie. There were lots of girls who loved him, but he was never a player. If anything, he had loads of friends who were girls, and they're all still friends to this day. I think he gets that from his mother, Andrea. Tyler and his mom absolutely loved each other, but they could also scream it out, which they did, in my office, on many occasions. He would come flying in, yelling, and then she would call me ten minutes later with her side of the story. It was very entertaining to watch.

Tyler came so far in his four years of high school. He truly put in the work. Of course, there were times when he shot himself in the foot, but that's what people do when they're learning to be grownups. Tyler knows when he's made a mistake, and he admits to it and makes the correction. He screwed up that freshman year so badly! But he really did learn how to do better, and then it became practice. That's what he's done when it comes to sports, to nutrition, to relationships, to everything he's interested in.

Tyler and I have remained close over the years. Just before his twenty-sixth birthday, his dad had been very sick. I called him and asked, "What are you doing for your birthday?" He told me he wasn't going to celebrate, so I took him out to eat. (Yes, Tyler celebrated his twenty-sixth birthday by having dinner with his guidance counselor.) While we were at dinner, he said, "Mrs. P, I have news that I know is really going to set you back." I don't watch much television, but my guilty or not-so-guilty pleasure has always been that *Bachelor/Bachelorette* series. I love to see different people doing these far-out things. Tyler told me he'd gone out to Los Angeles for his audition, and that he was so afraid he wasn't going to get cast. But, of course, he did.

When I first saw him on the show, I didn't know how far he'd make it or how much would happen. The way he came across at the very beginning, as this handsome model type, I didn't know if anyone, especially Hannah, would be able to see beyond the expectations. Also, in that first episode, he had on the ugliest pants I'd ever seen! They were way too short for him. I even texted him, saying, "Tyler, throw those pants in the trash can!"

As the show progressed, especially in the early episodes, it seemed like Hannah thought he was some kind of a player. I think it was hard to believe anyone could be that good-looking and kind and smart and not be an ass. But I think Tyler did a good job showing who he was, which is a truly nice guy. That made me really proud of him.

At his core, Tyler is a gentleman. He has a set of values and he applies them to whatever he does in his life. That's how he was raised by his mother, and that's always been something that's very important to him. When he meets people, he tries to engage them and see what he has in common with them to form a real connection, and he does it well.

My granddaughter, who was ten when Tyler's season of the show aired, is a huge *Bachelorette* fan, and without any prompting, Tyler brought her a rose. I think that made her whole year. Last winter, I was having a hard time getting my car started, and I called Tyler. He came over right away, in his sweaty workout T-shirt, and got my car out of the garage for me. He's always enthusiastic and willing to help. That's the person he is.

I still have an essay he wrote his senior year in English class about his plans for the future. He said he was going to be a quarterback in the NFL and that when he retired, he would come back to Florida and coach high school football. What I loved about the essay is that it wasn't about the glory of the job but the love of the sport. It was about following his truth and finding a way to give back at the same time. That is what's important to him, and I'm happy to say that has not changed.

4

TAKE A CHANCE

My Time on The Bachelorette

The first time I ever watched *The Bachelorette* was with my ex-girlfriend Mariah. It was JoJo Fletcher's season, and at one point, I turned to Mariah and said, "If you break up with me, I'm gonna go on that show." It was a complete joke. But I guess there was also some truth to it, because a couple years later, I applied.

It was the summer of 2018, and I was home in Jupiter, Florida, getting my general contractor's license. One day, I was taking a break from studying, and I saw something online about applying for the WWE.

"Should I apply for this?" I texted my friends. I could just picture myself in a little Speedo throwing chairs and shit.

"Yeah, you'd be great for it!" they shot back. So I applied.

"You should see what else you can apply for," one of my friends suggested.

I searched around, and a post about auditioning for *The Bachelor* popped up. *Why not?* I thought, so I applied for that, too.

I went about making a ridiculous profile, including the douchiest picture of myself that I could find—this shot of me posing by the water on the beach, with my shirt lifted up over my abs like a crop top. When I actually took the photo, I was joking around with some friends and I wasn't taking myself seriously. It was a good picture, but it was also totally goofy. But for this, it somehow seemed perfect.

Next, I wrote absurd responses to their questions. Here's an actual quote from my application: "When I come out of that limo with Boyz II Men singing 'Can You Stand the Rain' a cappella, and they let me bust out my part and spin my lady around when I meet her, not only will she know I am the most eligible bachelor, but all the girls watching around America will know as well." Looking back, I can't believe I wrote half the stuff I did. I showed my friends the finished application, and they were like, "Dude, this is amazing." And then I sent it in and went back to studying.

I truly didn't expect anything to come of it, but then a week later, the casting directors hit me back. They asked me to send them more photos and videos showing who I am and what I do. Two weeks went by, and I didn't get around to it. I was busy studying for my general contractor's license, and if I'm being honest, at that point, I didn't really care. I didn't think I would actually get on the show, so none of it felt real to me. Another week went by, and the casting people followed up to say, "Can you Skype us?" So maybe they were interested after all.

Before the call, I set up all this lighting in my room so I would look good on camera. (If there's one thing I've learned from modeling, it's that lighting is important.) I had two different lamps pointing directly at me. When the time came to talk with them, the lights were basically the only things that worked. My computer broke. The connection wouldn't work. So I propped up my phone and used that as the camera, but the feed wasn't showing the picture, which meant I couldn't see myself. I didn't know how I looked, how my hair looked, if I had any boogers. Finally, somehow, we did the interview and I guess they liked me, because a few weeks later, they sent me down to Fort Lauderdale for an actual, in-person audition.

As soon as I arrived, the casting directors sat me down in a little room and started talking. Even at the interview, I didn't think I had a good chance of making it onto the show, and I wasn't taking it too seriously. But I guess they *still* liked me, because after that, they sent me to L.A. for the final interview.

The callbacks took place on a weekend, at a hotel in L.A.

I remember I wore a white button-down and a blazer with elbow patches, paired with jeans and brown loafers, no socks. I've never worn socks with loafers, and I never will. It's a South Florida thing.

The whole weekend was a complete whirlwind. I could never tell if I was making a good impression or whether the people I was talking to liked me. I remember trying to keep it all as lighthearted as possible, joking around, even dancing at one point after admitting I was almost a dance minor in college. True story. My mentality was still that there was no way I was going to make it on the show, so why not have a great time and just bring my normal, goofy energy. If they liked me, then I wanted them to like me for being my authentic self, and because I knew I wouldn't ever be able to act any different, even if I was on TV.

Once the auditions were over, I still had no clue what they thought of me. I couldn't tell if my big personality had come across well, or if they had actually liked my sense of humor (or my moves). But they sent me off without any indication of whether or not I'd made it, and just said they'd be in touch soon.

With the audition behind me, I had one night left in L.A., and even though I was out there by myself, I wanted to make the most of this strange experience. I was completely finished with my casting experience, but I made the decision to extend my time in L.A. so I could appreciate all that California had to offer on my own.

I had booked my flight home early the next morning, but I decided I would go out and have fun in L.A.

Now, I'm not a big pot smoker. I was an athlete for my whole life, and I was never into drugs. But recreational marijuana had been legalized in California, and I thought this would be the perfect chance to go see one of these dispensaries everyone had been talking about. So I went to one—it looked like an Apple store for weed products—and asked the woman working there how much of this gummy I should take.

"I take twenty milligrams," she told me.

This woman barely cleared my chest, I must have been twice the size of her. So I figured if she took twenty milligrams, I could afford to take thirty. And that's what I did.

My plan was to get a little buzz on, go to the Santa Monica Pier, and then have a nice dinner by myself. I figured I was out on this wild adventure, and even though I still didn't believe I'd get cast for *The Bachelorette*, I was going to enjoy this wild experience in L.A. now that casting was over and I was out in California on my own. I made it down to the beach, where I called my buddy who smokes a lot. He said, "I take twenty milligrams to get high and thirty milligrams to get *baked.*"

Oops.

I'd already eaten three gummies, or the equivalent of thirty milligrams.

For a while, I felt fine.

Then all of a sudden it hit me.

Oh my god. I am stoned.

I called an Uber to take me back to the hotel and waited on the beach alone, surrounded by beautiful scenery. There were bright streetlights and multimillion-dollar houses all around me—there was nothing scary about this neighborhood. But I was so paranoid from the gummies that I convinced myself someone was going to jump me. I darted around, hiding in shadows and peeking around corners until my car arrived.

On the ride back, I grew even more paranoid, this time worrying that my Uber driver might be secretly working for *The Bachelorette,* and that they were spying on me after the audition was over. Of course, that wasn't happening, but the logic made sense in my paranoid state and I didn't want to give anything away or make a bad impression. Naturally, I decided the safest move would be not to speak. My driver kept trying to make small talk, but I was determined to ride in complete silence. I can only imagine what she must have thought.

I arrived at the hotel—still completely stoned.

When I finally found my room, I immediately crawled into bed and hid under the blankets. I swear I heard someone knocking at the door, but it might have just been my paranoia. Either way, I didn't answer, and I was careful not to make a sound. I stayed hidden under those covers until morning.

In my panic the night before, I had forgotten to set an alarm, but somehow I woke up at 5:30 a.m., thirty minutes before I had to leave.

I raced to the airport, hopped on my plane, and booked it out of there. I spent the whole flight home laughing at myself about my paranoia the night before. I couldn't believe that even though I had been completely done with casting and on my own time before my big night out, I had still been so nervous that I would get caught. Sitting on the plane, I finally had time to reflect on my audition, still thinking that my chances of getting on the show were impossibly low. But I knew I'd done my best and been myself. And at the very least, I now had a hilarious story from L.A. that I could bring home to my friends.

After I got back from L.A., about a month went by without a word.

On February 14—Valentine's Day—I was working a modeling job for Cartier, for their store in Miami. My job was to be a door boy, which meant I stood at the entrance greeting people, wearing a little red suit and serving champagne while holding a heart-shaped box of chocolates. I looked like some sort of bellhop from a romantic comedy, as imagined by Wes Anderson. It was quite a look. The ensemble even had a little black hat to top it all off.

So there I was, working that job, knowing the call would be coming soon. I kept my phone in my pocket the whole time I was working the door, just hoping it would be good news. Finally, my phone buzzed, and I saw it was a call from California. I knew that had to be it.

"Hey, this is Margot," said the voice on the other end of the line, "and we're so excited to have you as part of the show!"

From that moment on, I was like, *Let's go.* I was ready for anything. But before I could do anything else, I actually had to figure out what this show was all about.

First, I watched Colton Underwood's season with my mom and my grandparents. I remember watching hometowns, where the final contestants traveled back to their hometowns to introduce Colton to their families. My grandparents were like, "What is this show you're going on?" My mom, on the other hand, was all about it.

My dad watched a lot of it with us, too. As we made our way through Colton's season, I was careful not to watch any of the episodes that featured a lot of Hannah. I didn't want to form an opinion of her before I actually met her. But my dad watched them all. And from what he saw, he thought that we were meant to be.

All along, he was like, "That's your girl, that's your girl." He was convinced.

As the show got closer, I struggled with whether to go through with it, because my dad's health wasn't great. At the time, he was only a month out from his intestinal surgery. I wanted to be on the show, of course, but a part of me was worried about leaving him behind when he might need me.

"I've got Dad," my mom told me. "I'll take care of him. We'll be fine."

Still, I felt so guilty. My dad could barely walk back then, and who was going to help run his company? I didn't want to put more on his plate by going on national television. But both my parents insisted that this was the right thing to do.

I didn't own anything nice to wear—half my wardrobe was board shorts and surf shirts—and none of my clothes fit, because I was in the process of transitioning from a 250-pound athlete to a 210-pound model. So a couple of weeks before I left for the show, while in New York for a modeling job, I walked up and down Fifth Avenue and bought a bunch of clothes. I got some suits at Zara and made sure everything was a little tight-fitting, because I was trying to make it look tailored.

Dressing for the show was hard, but I tried to make it fun. When it came to my clothes, I brought my Florida taste to everything. Normally, I don't wear suits. So I thought, what do those people wear when they're yachting in Miami? (Never mind that I couldn't even get a job *working* on a yacht, let alone own one.) I tried to give everything that Miami vibe—gray or khaki pants, light blues that reminded me of the water, bright corals and teals. I wanted my looks to pop. Before I left, my best friend Katie gave me a gift, a light-blue tie with different colors of flowers on it, and told me to wear it when I was sure I really liked Hannah. I wound up breaking it out for the rose ceremony right after hometowns.

Going into *The Bachelorette*, I had no expectations. I didn't know if I would actually fall in love, but I knew I was open to it. I knew it was an amazing experience, and I wanted to make the most of it. I put on my best suit—after I bought all those clothes at Zara, my mom got me a Brooks Brothers gift card so I could have at least one nice suit, and that was what I wore for the first night. I was juiced up and ready to go.

My hotel room faced the back of the building, where I had a view of the pool and also the parking lot. This meant I could see everyone lining up to go in the limos. I saw all the other guys, in their outfits and all that, coming out in groups and getting into the cars. Five p.m. had come and gone, but all I could do was watch and wait. I wondered when it would be my turn.

I waited for what felt like forever, standing at the window, practicing what I wanted to say to her. Finally, a producer came and got me. The time had come at last.

On the way to the house, I met all these guys—Garrett, Mike,

Jed, and Dylan—and tried to make small talk. One by one, I watched them do their entrances.

When we sat outside the gate in the limo line, I was like, *I got it.* But then as we pulled up to the house, my heart dropped.

As the limo approached, I could see her.

I watched all the guys go out, one by one, until finally, it was my turn.

All I could think was, *Holy shit. This is about to happen.* I stepped out of the limo, and there she was, in this shimmering gold dress with sequins all over it. And I'm like, *Damn. This is real.* It was all very intimidating. From the moment I opened the car door, there were a thousand lights everywhere. It was blinding; nothing could ever prepare you for that moment. During those days in the hotel room, I'd rehearsed what I wanted to say to Hannah a million times. For the past twenty-four hours, the words were running through my mind constantly. But as soon as I was actually face-to-face with her, I started talking out of the side of my neck. I said whatever the hell I said, I hugged her, and then I walked inside, thinking, *What the hell just happened?*

That first night at the mansion, I looked around at all the other guys and felt intimidated. First off, they all looked sharp as hell. Plus, everyone seemed so successful. They all had dope jobs—a golf pro, an ex–pro basketball player, a pilot . . . I had no money compared to these dudes. Their bios are like, "John Paul Jones, Finance" and "Dylan, App Creator." There were some real hitters in there. Meanwhile, I'm working for my dad.

The whole time I kept thinking: *Everyone is good-looking, and they all have their shit together. I'm good-looking, but I'm a mess! These guys are the real deal.*

To make matters worse, that first night, I hardly even saw Hannah, never mind talked to her. There were some moments when I could have said, "I'm going to find her," but I thought it was better to wait my turn so I wouldn't step on anyone's toes. I was also dead sober, because I didn't want to drink the first time I met her. I wanted to be sharp and clear and make sure I was bringing my best self.

As I sat there still waiting for my chance, the next thing I knew, Chris Harrison, the show's host, said it was time for the rose ceremony. *Great*, I thought. *I haven't gotten to talk to her. At all. Night one, and I'm definitely going home. How embarrassing.* But then, as Hannah started to give out the roses, she called the names of some of the other dudes who hadn't seen her, either, and I knew that I at least had a chance.

Being on *The Bachelorette* brought me out of my comfort zone in a lot of ways. Right away, the lights and the cameras and the set were like nothing I'd ever experienced. But I heard someone say, "If you make it through night one, you can make it through anything." Midway through the rose ceremony, she called my name. I was safe. I did everything you shouldn't do that night (except the staying sober part), but I got lucky.

Here's a big life lesson from my early days on the show: If you feel inclined to do something, go do it. I'm not saying to go break any laws or anything. But don't listen to people who tell you how you should or shouldn't act when it's something you feel you have to do.

If I could do it all over again, I would just barge into the room and say, "We gotta talk." If Hannah was upset, I would find a way to make it better. I've learned that sometimes the only way to make something happen is to do it yourself. If you feel something, if you believe it in your gut, just trust that it's right.

After that first night at the mansion, I was like, *I will never let another opportunity pass me by again.* The rest of the time I was there, I decided to take the initiative. That's another lesson: Take a chance. Even if it seems like a long shot, try to see what happens.

There's a saying that my middle school teachers loved: "Shoot for the stars; if you don't make it, you'll land on the moon." When I was younger, I thought it was so cheesy. (And if I'm being honest, I still do.) But it always stuck with me, and now I see there's a lot of truth to it. You need to give yourself permission to go after what you want, even if at first it might feel like a long shot. You see that girl or that guy at the bar and you want to get to know them? Go talk to them. You see a job or a gig that interests you? Apply for it. The worst thing you can do is not try. You'll never know if you don't go.

Being on *The Bachelorette* helped me find my confidence. In the early days, I felt insecure and preferred to stay inside my shell, afraid to talk to anybody. Between the cameras and the other guys, there was a lot of pressure and I kind of froze. As I said, I was intimidated by the other men at first, but the more time I spent with everyone, the more I realized that I could blow these dudes away, having learned so much and grown so much in recent years. When I saw everyone interacting on a group date, it gave me more confidence, because I saw that their connections weren't as strong as ours. The more I leaned into that feeling, the more confident I got that I could really be in this thing, and the more I realized that I was ready for a real commitment and that Hannah and I had a genuine connection.

The show forced me to stick up for myself and others. In my everyday life, I don't like to argue, I don't like to fight. But growing up, I was always taught that you should stick up for those who can't stick up for themselves. There were times on the show when some of the other guys would talk shit about Hannah or do things that upset her. That got me frustrated. Hannah didn't deserve that. Moreover, if she was upset, she would cancel a date, and that took away opportunities for everybody.

If you watched Hannah's season, you'll remember Cam. He was trouble from day one. He crashed dates; he inserted himself where he didn't belong. Hannah needed all the time she had to figure out what was right for her, and I wasn't about to let some other guy get in the way of that. I saw that if I didn't stand up to Cam, he would continue to soak up all of Hannah's time and make it harder for her to get to know everyone else.

In my eyes, a confident person doesn't need to push others down in order to make themselves look better. When it came to Cam, I decided to let him know exactly how I felt. "Don't fuck with Hannah's time, and don't fuck with my time," I told him. "And if you do, then we'll have some problems." The moment I said it, everyone's eyes went wide. I'd been silent up until this point, but that was the moment I first stepped up to make my values known to the group. From that point forward, everyone knew who I was.

Just when I thought I was fully out of my comfort zone, *The Bachelorette* made me confront some of my phobias. One day in Amsterdam, the date card read, "Get ready to ride off into the sunset." Right off the bat, I didn't like the sound of it. I was not going to ride a goddamn horse. When I was a kid, a horse kicked my friend in the face, and ever since then, I do not mess with them. Period.

I went to meet Hannah, and right away she said, "I have an awesome date for us—I can't wait to show you!" We turned the corner to see two *giant* Clydesdales. That's right. Not just a horse, this was a damn Clydesdale. They're massive and terrifying. I wanted no part of this. But I didn't have much of a choice at that point, so I gritted my teeth and climbed up into the saddle. *Not* riding the horse didn't seem to be an option if I wanted to spend this time with Hannah.

For the rest of the date, we tried to rip these horses through the city. I wanted to go right, but my horse went left. I wanted to go forward, so the horse went back. I hated the horse; the horse hated me. The whole time we were riding, I barely talked to Hannah because I was in fear for my life. At one point, we got off the horses to take a break, and my legs were shaking from how hard I'd been squeezing the horse with my thighs.

At least after that date, I knew nothing could be worse. I'd already ridden a horse, so no date could be harder for me to cope with. I was in the clear. Or at least I thought I was. But Hannah's and my final date proved the world was out to get me. I had to ride a horse again. I tried to get on the horse, and it started running away from me. That second time around, though, I was better prepared. Having one horse-riding date already behind me gave me the confidence to do it again. This time, I actually conquered the horse. We walked slow and tight, and I was able to keep it together. Don't get me wrong, horses still freak me out. But sometimes confronting your fears really does make them better. I've gone riding again since then, and now I don't have that same terror; and even though I hope I never *have* to ride a horse again, I know that I can.

The absolute biggest thing I learned from the show—bigger than standing up for myself and Hannah, and even bigger than how to ride a horse—was the way it taught me to open up. Before the show, I struggled to be vulnerable. When I went on dates, I relied on small talk—here's a little bit about me, here's a little bit about you. It was very surface-level. But I was always afraid to show the deeper parts of myself. There were some dark family things in my past, as well as some insecurities, that I found really hard to share with someone new.

It took my ex-girlfriend Mariah nearly a year to learn the same things about me that Hannah got to know within weeks. But dating on the show gives you no choice—everything moves at an accelerated timeline that forces you to dive in deep and throw down all your cards on the table. It's extreme speed dating. You have only a few weeks to figure out the answers to all these big questions, so you can't afford to hold anything back.

Part of the reason Hannah and I hit it off—and why she first said she was impressed by me—was because I locked in when I was with her. When we were together, I did two things: I gave her my full attention, and I let her see who I really was. In this accelerated environment, opening up came more naturally to me. When you're on a date with someone you really want to get to know, that's the only way to be. Hannah told me, "You always find a way to make a moment happen between just the two of us, even with all these people around."

Hannah was good at asking questions, which also encouraged me to open up. In all our conversations, she would manage to pull a lot out of me. She just kept pulling and pulling, especially when it came to the tougher subjects. I knew that if I couldn't open up to her, she wouldn't keep me around, so I told her everything I could to help show her who I am. Once I started having those conversations, I saw that opening up to someone didn't hurt—it actually felt really good.

It allowed for a much deeper relationship, and it made our relationship real and true, right off the bat.

That's a lesson I've taken into my dating life now; I put a lot out there fairly quickly. I try to be completely open and myself right away, because I don't want to waste their time, and I don't want to waste my time. It's better to see what everyone's about so you can see if you're on the same page. When I go on a date with someone, I want to understand who she is and where she's coming from. Sometimes your cards match up, and sometimes they don't. When you share yourself with somebody, you build a bond, you build a trust, you build a comfort level. It allows you to look at them differently and connect with them more.

One of my favorite questions to ask is "If a dollar never mattered, what would you do?" I'll ask about their families—do they get along with their siblings, what was home like, what was it like when they were growing up? I'll ask about their passions—what inspires them, what brought them to live in the place where they are now? I ask the questions that I know I would want someone to ask about me.

Those tough conversations, those real ones, are things I always struggled with and shied away from, because I didn't want people to know about my past. I was afraid to open up about my parents, about my partying, about the mistakes I've made in my life and relationships. But the more I shared things, the more I learned about myself, too. By sharing who I had become, I came to understand that I didn't have to be that person anymore who made those mistakes. It's possible to learn and grow from the past, and then move on.

Being on *The Bachelorette* helped me open up in other parts of my life, too. The conversation I had with my dad before hometowns was one of the best I've ever had with him. My dad and I can talk about a lot of things, and I get his advice on sports and business, but heart-to-hearts have never come easily to us. When I was dating Mariah, I never talked to my dad about my relationship. If he asked me about it, I'd just offer something like, "Yeah, we're cool," without going into any details. But with Hannah, I felt compelled to tell him everything. During those conversations, we also talked about our lives, how much I missed him, and his health. I was able to answer all his questions about Hannah as I got ready to take this next big step in my life. At the time, I already knew I was going to propose to her if I got the chance. We even talked about what love was. One of the coolest things about it was that since it happened on camera, I'll have that conversation saved forever.

Before the show, I wasn't comfortable having emotional conversations. I didn't really know how to. But once I had some practice and saw the value of being vulnerable in a romantic relationship, I found I could apply it to different parts of my life. Don't get me wrong, I'm still learning how to do this. Sometimes my pride still gets in the way of me opening up, because I don't want to get hurt again. But I've also seen how good it is for me when I do it. So I'm working on it.

Progress isn't a straight line. Whether it's learning to open up, or really anything you're working on in your life, often it's two steps forward, one step back. Don't get discouraged if you backslide on your journey toward making a change. Just keep pushing forward.

On one of our one-on-one dates, Hannah and I went lobstering, which was not at all like the lobstering I do in Florida. When I'm with my brothers and my friends lobstering, let's just say it's grittier and a lot less romantic. But it was still a cool thing to do together, because it gave us the space to kick back and talk. That night, over dinner, she asked me, "Why are you really on this show?" Up until that point, she had her guard up, because she thought I was just on the show to get attention or to help with my career. "You're a model, you do other things—what are you after?" she asked. She also thought I was a fuckboy and a player, something she assumed because of the way I look and where I'm from. In her defense, that was part of my past persona, but by that point it was something I had completely outgrown. Still, her image of me gave her pause for obvious reasons, so I had to open up to show her the man I had become.

I was dead honest with her. I told her, "Yes, I was a fuckboy. But then I got in a serious relationship and realized how much I love romance and how much I love finding a good person and actually being with that person." I told her the truth—that a real connection is so much more important to me than anything else. I told her that I had already messed up once in a relationship by being reckless and that I wasn't ever going to do that again.

I also told her about my dad. I told her how he'd almost died a few months before and how I almost didn't come on the show because of it. I shared that I felt tremendous guilt about leaving him, but that my guilt had gone away the more I got to know her, because it felt like I was meant to be there.

That conversation did a lot to bring us together. It's not that I said anything that was so profound; I was just honest with her. I was genuine. That's something I've come to understand about opening up and sharing your true self with people: You don't need to make some big proclamations; you just have to be yourself. When you show someone who you really are and share what you believe and what you're looking for, it's meaningful because it's true.

After that night, I was on cloud nine. The whole thing was getting me in my feels. That's what the show does—they put you in these intense situations that are so amazing that everything you feel is multiplied by a thousand. After lobstering, Hannah and I went to a concert, surrounded by hundreds of screaming people. We got up onto the stage together, where I remember looking Hannah in the eyes—even with all these other people around us—and feeling like we were the only two people on Earth.

• • • • •

Of course, in the end, Hannah didn't pick me. People always ask me how I felt when Hannah ultimately didn't choose me. Did I regret any of the things I said? Did some part of me wish I hadn't put myself out there? The answer is no. In fact, it's the opposite. When you let it all out there, you have no regrets. I figured: *If it works, it works. If it don't, then it don't.* But I wouldn't let it not work out because I didn't give it my all.

Walking away from the show, what made everything okay was that I knew I gave it my all. Hannah had stronger feelings for another guy, and that was that. But I knew it wasn't for lack of trying on my part. If I'd held something back, I would have been filled with "but what if I'd done this?" But now, I don't have those doubts. I left no stone unturned. I had no shoulda-coulda-wouldas, because I knew that I put it all out there. I put everything on the line, I threw my heart out on the table (which I'd never really done before), and that was what allowed me to walk away with peace.

That's the last thing I learned on the show: Don't hold back. Tell that person how you feel about them. Tell them who you really are. Don't be afraid to say what you're thinking or to ask for what you want. Put yourself out there, do something uncomfortable, and give it your all. No matter what happens, you can go forward knowing you have no regrets. You might be surprised at what you can do.

The Real Tyler:

· ·

ACCORDING TO HIS FRIEND MATT

The first time I met Tyler was on campus at Wake Forest, when he was moving into my old freshman dorm. My very first impression was just that I was in shock over how big he was. He looked like a full-blown college quarterback. I liked him immediately. People from Florida have good vibes. They worry less, and they're good people persons. I was like, "He is the truth, and we're going to be nice."

When he first arrived, of course, he hadn't made friends yet, and he was trying to figure out the lay of the land. Some friends and I were leaving for South Carolina for the weekend. We would go down there often, to the University of South Carolina, because everyone hated football players at Wake. People didn't come to Wake Forest for the athletics; they came to meet their future spouses and to be doctors and lawyers and other high-paying jobs. So we would head to USC for parties.

As we were gearing up to leave, we saw Tyler and asked, "Hey, T.C., want to head down there with us?" He said yes right away. I'm super spontaneous, and I immediately liked that he was, too. That weekend was like everything you imagine a college-party weekend would be. (It also gave him the most unrealistic expectation of what college was.) We still talk about it to this day. That was the start of our friendship.

We weren't the best of friends in college yet, but we were always homies.

When I first moved to New York, I rented a room in this apartment on the Upper West Side. It was tiny, but it was affordable, and it was in NYC. We were really in the action. T.C. was trying to pursue his modeling career, and it made sense for him to stay in New York while he figured that out. My room was hardly big enough for one person, let alone two. But I think for both of us, being athletes, having brothers, we were used to just making whatever situation work. So I told him to stay with me.

Somehow, we made an eight-by-frickin'-ten-foot room work for almost six months. That was a long time to share that tiny room, but it was so much fun. People used to say I had a bunk bed; it was not a bunk bed. It was a lofted double bed. I had a *huge* beanbag underneath it, and T.C. slept on that. I don't care what he says, I know how comfortable that beanbag was. Any time one of us lay down on that thing, it was lights out. He made me throw it away when we got to our new apartment, but I know he was as sad as I was to see it go.

One day, when Tyler had been living at the tiny apartment for around five months, one of my roommates figured out who he was. Because he had been on TV, she figured he must have been a millionaire who was making all this money and was holding out on everyone. She cornered me in the living room. "I know who's staying in your room," she said. "He's not on the lease. And he should be paying more money." She was like, "You can either pay more rent or I'm going to go to the leasing office to tell on you!" My roommate and I started going back and forth—she's telling me we need to pay more, and I'm telling her she never cleans the kitchen or the toilet. Looking back, it wasn't a big deal, but it was the principle of the thing.

When it came to the walls in this apartment, to say they were paper-thin is an exaggeration—there may as well have been no wall. The whole time this exchange was going on, Tyler was on the bean-bag, holding his breath, listening to us hash it out. Finally, I got back in the room, and Tyler looked at me, and I saw he was smiling. "It looks like we're moving out of here!" he said. We were dying laugh-ing. We moved out two weeks later, into the building we live in now, which is one of the nicer, newer buildings in New York. Looking back on that whole situation, that we could go from sleeping literally on top of each other to living in such a nice, new apartment building is funny to me. But in a way, I guess, we're still on top of each other. I still use his bathroom. We still hang out in his bedroom. In some ways, nothing has changed.

One thing I love about Tyler is when you ask him how he's doing, he's not just like, "Good," or "All right." He actually tells you how he's feeling. He's like, "Bro, I'm dealing with x, y, z." There's no song and dance pretending he's fine. We get to the root of a deep, intel-lectual conversation quickly. He makes me open up. His willingness to be open and share everything in his life makes you want to do anything for him.

In the time I've known him, he's grown into a man. He's that father figure that his younger brothers need. He's just a grown-up. When I look back to college, we were just kids. He was the life of the party, super athletic, everyone wanted to be around him, funny.

None of that stuff's changed, but the way I look at him now is more like a thought leader. A person who's supporting his family. He's driven, he's motivated, he runs a construction company, he's doing so many things. It's encouraging to see people step into their potential and fully take on everything they're capable of doing. In life, a lot of people fold, but T.C.'s got some big shoulders.

When COVID-19 hit, and the stay-at-home order happened, he opened up his house in Florida to all of us. He didn't have to do that; he had so much to deal with, and yet he had everyone, all his friends who made up the Quarantine Crew, in his house. I don't know anyone else who would do that. But that's who he is. That's who his mom was, and that's who he is. He just wants to take care of everybody.

A few years back, Tyler was in New York trying out for an NFL team, where he was going to showcase his stats or whatever. When I heard he was coming to town, I said, "You're welcome to stay with me." I also told him, "I have some ideas to run by you." He could've done anything that weekend—he could've gone out, chased girls, partied in the city, whatever—and instead, we hashed out the idea for what ABC Food Tours would become. He went to meet restaurant owners with me, and we strategized what we could do. I remember thinking, *I don't know what's going to happen, but I know this idea is going to be something great.*

We wanted our voices to matter, we wanted kids to be excited to interact with us, and happily, it all just came together. We love interacting with students. I feel like I see myself in a lot of these kids. I've been the beneficiary of somebody taking the time and investing in my life, and it's paid back tenfold. Those opportunities we're providing, you never know how that's going to impact somebody's life, what it might help drive them to aspire to and be.

When it comes to his fame, hell yeah, I would've predicted it! In a way, I'm surprised it took this long, because he's such a character. That's just who he is. He doesn't even have to try, he's completely himself. I'm just happy that everyone's gotten a taste of who he is as a person. Those are the people you hope are elevated and have a platform, because they encourage and inspire people.

As for social media or tabloids, some people look at things through a narrow lens, but that's not having perspective. *The Bachelorette* was a chapter in his life, but it's not his book, it's not his story. That was an isolated time, an isolated event.

It's like, when I was a kid, I used to ask my mom questions like, "How do you spell *caterpillar*?" And she would say, "Go look it up." Which was annoying, because I wanted her to just tell me how to spell it. But when you actually look into the knowledge you want, it leads you to more information. You see how to spell a word, but you might also discover that caterpillars turn into butterflies. It's easy to just believe what you hear without knowing the full story. Anyone who gets to know the real Tyler would have the same admiration and respect for him that I do.

One thing Tyler's taught me is how to be selfless. He's the last person he takes into consideration when he's weighing any thought, action, or idea. He'll be like, "Yo, this could be good for this person! This would be good for that person! This would be good for my dad. This would be good for my brother . . ."

His natural inclination is to help everyone else. What he doesn't always realize is that doing so creates allies all across the board. He empowers them, uplifts them, gives them a platform, puts them on their game. He empowers everyone around him to be the best they can be. It's like, "Why do you do that?" But that's just who he is.

5

BE RESPECTFUL

How I Became an Accidental Feminist Icon

The whole time I was on *The Bachelorette*, I kept saying the same phrase over and over: "This is our opportunity, but it's Hannah's story." The way I saw it, the show—the whole experience—was all for her. We, the guys, had an amazing opportunity being on the show and getting to know Hannah, but no matter what, whether she picked you or not, it was all about Hannah's journey. Whenever someone else on the show tried to take that away from Hannah, by stealing the spotlight or tearing her down, I knew in my heart that it wasn't right. My attitude was: respect her time, respect everyone else's time, and let's try to make it the best experience possible.

Near the end of the season, we all traveled to Latvia, where Hannah went bungee jumping with Garrett, one of the other guys, on a one-on-one date. Apparently, it's a Latvian pastime for couples to bungee jump naked, so in keeping with tradition, they both wore only their underwear. Some of the other guys had a problem with that, Luke in particular. He was fuming.

"Her body is a temple, and to expose it to anyone who isn't her husband . . . that was a slap in my face," he said.

I didn't agree.

"I actually respect and love that she went for it," I replied. "She's making her own decisions . . . let her go have those experiences." I really ripped into him. Again, this was her story. If she wanted to go bungee jumping butt-ass naked, let her! It was her body, her life, her dream. Who were we to tell her what to do or how to live? She wasn't in a committed relationship with any of us. Why would any of us try to take away from her experience due to our own insecurities?

As soon as that episode aired, the press started calling me a feminist icon. I was dubbed "Respectful Woke King" and all these stupid nicknames. I am a feminist, of course, and believe that all genders should have equal rights in all ways. But even today, I don't think anything I did or said was worthy of that much praise. I mean, was it *that* big a deal that I thought Hannah should be free to do whatever she wanted with her own body? I was just standing up for her right to make her own decisions. I was only saying something from the heart. Something that, to me, seemed so obvious.

I didn't think I was making some big feminist statement. I just looked at it like, if you love someone, don't you want them to have fun and enjoy themselves? Who am I to judge a woman's choices? She needed to figure shit out for herself. Who am I to say what any person can or can't do, especially if it has nothing to do with me? Honestly, I felt the same way when it came to *all* her choices, including who she did or didn't want to sleep with. At one point, I told her, "Look, I don't care what you do with any of the other guys. You need to do whatever you need to do in order to figure out where your heart is." And I meant it. If she wound up with me, I wanted her to know that she had zero regrets. That she had lived the entire experience of the show and explored every avenue that her heart led her down.

All along, Hannah and I had this super-hot chemistry. We made out everywhere; we had that part all figured out. Leading up to our date in the fantasy suite, she told me she made up her mind that she didn't want to have sex.

Now, as anyone who's watched the show will know, everything about the fantasy suite (including the name!) holds a connotation of sex. But for a cast member, it's so much more than that. It's one of the most important times on the show. The night in the fantasy suite is the only uninterrupted period of time when you're completely alone and not on camera. Throughout the other weeks, you might get quick breaks here and there, but the fantasy suite is the biggest stretch of time when you can see whether everything really works. (Needless to say, if you fall asleep in the fantasy suite, you're not meant to be together.)

During that night together, we hooked up and it kept getting steamy, but I kept pumping the brakes. "I just want to talk more," I said. I told her I had already made a promise to her that we wouldn't. "No means no," I said. I wanted to honor that, and I didn't want her to do something she might regret later. We had the best night—just hanging out, talking and connecting. We really opened up and poured into each other, tackling so many big topics and sharing so much of ourselves. The fact that we could easily talk all night was what made me think, *Holy shit, this could be it for me.* I was genuinely upset when I saw the sun coming up, because I knew our time to-gether was almost at an end.

Hannah and I had a meaningful night, without having sex. It was great and, I thought, a perfectly normal thing to do. But again, the response from viewers was so big.

A lot of things came out of my experience on the show, a big one being an inadvertent and unexpected passion for trying to help correct our dating culture. What is consent, and why isn't it universally understood? What does being a "good guy" really entail? Are things so bad in our culture that what I did on the show was worthy of so much praise?

If what went down with Hannah and me inspired more people to talk about consent, then I'm grateful for that. But in my eyes, the reaction to my part in that conversation was completely unwarranted. All I did was listen to her when she said she didn't want to have sex—that was it. No is no, and I was just honoring what Hannah told me. I did what was right, but I don't deserve a prize for doing that. This should be *normal*. We shouldn't even bat an eye at it.

All along, I kept thinking, *What did I even do that was such a big deal?!* All I did was treat someone the way that everyone deserves to be treated. If that's all it takes to be a "Respectful Woke King," it's not just sad—it's scary.

Here are a few of the headlines and taglines that ran near the end of the show:

"SOMEHOW, *THE BACHELORETTE* JUST DELIVERED A MASTER CLASS IN CONSENT"
—*MARIE CLAIRE*

"THE BACHELORETTE FINALE WINNER WAS FEMINISM"
—NBC NEWS

"IS TYLER C THE MOST FEMINIST CONTESTANT EVER?"

—THE LIST

"TYLER CAMERON IS ONE OF THE GOOD ONES"

—*PAPER*

"TYLER CAMERON IS A FEMINIST HERO!"

—PRETTY MUCH EVERYONE ELSE

The day we shot the *After the Final Rose* special, I was standing in the parking lot after we wrapped, saying my goodbyes, when the president of ABC drove by me. She hopped out of her car and said, "You're the feminist icon this show needed." Now, I wasn't about to argue with her, so I just said, "Thank you," and took a bunch of pictures with her kids. To be clear, I do think it made for good entertainment. The conflict between me and Luke having such polar opposite views of the same issue—he was old-school and conservative in his ways, while I thought Hannah should have been able to do whatever she wanted to do—you couldn't have written it better. But being good on TV does not an icon make.

To this day, my boys are like, "You should want to be called a feminist icon!" And I do! Of course I do. It's great. But my point is that it's unwarranted. Maybe I'm a feminist because I wanted Hannah to be who she was and defended her when she made her own decisions. But if I'm a feminist *icon*, then we have a problem. I gave Hannah the space to be herself and listened to what she told me. That should be the norm! Suddenly, just respecting someone's wishes is a master class on consent? That only shows you how fucked up our dating culture is. No wonder we're all out here having such a hard time.

Everything I said or did was based on one simple principle: respect. When it comes to relationships, respect is everything. It's consent. It's asking questions. It's listening to what someone has to say. It's respecting people's boundaries. It's treating the people you date the same way you would treat your best, closest friends.

Now, if Hannah and I were married and she went bungee jumping naked with some guy, that might be different. But on the show, we were all dating and competing against one another, and Hannah needed to do what she had to do to figure out what was best for her.

Our society talks so much about women and empowerment and lifting one another up, but then it seems we rarely practice what we preach. Another thing that makes me sad is that every time I'm seen with a woman, the same terrible cycle happens. Everyone—fans, the media—rips the woman apart and tears her down. The shit people send me and the comments I've seen online? They're downright nasty. I can't believe people feel compelled to say the things they do. It makes me feel terrible for these women, who don't deserve to be put under that light. They're just living their lives, trying to date and be normal.

As you can probably tell, when people talk trash about any woman I'm seen with, it really upsets me. I was spotted getting a piece of pizza with a girl and everyone jumped all over it. The whole internet started going through all her social media accounts, looking through old photos and pulling up posts from years before. Here's the thing: you can never form a real opinion about someone from what you see in tabloids, and you can never know what they're really like based on social media. Oftentimes, in person, people are completely different from how they seem. Someone might seem shallow or unpleasant based on their social media feed, and then in real life, they're actually the sweetest, kindest, most caring person.

When people comment about a person's appearance—saying maybe someone had her nose done or her boobs done, or when they comment on their clothing—it drives me wild. Who cares? Maybe that's not your personal preference, but it's not your body. If wearing a certain thing or doing a certain thing makes someone happy, who are we to judge their choices? Whatever another person does to feel good is none of my business. Everyone is fighting their own battles. You never know what another person is going through. So be kind.

I grew up in Florida, where everyone wore thong bikinis, and then I went to college at Wake Forest, where people wore shorts over their bathing suits, even in the water. People have different styles and different beliefs, and that's okay. No one way is right. But people tearing one another down because of what one of them chooses to do with their body is ridiculous. If it isn't hurting anyone, what does it matter?

The *Bachelor* fan base can be amazing, but just like all social media, the culture around it isn't always positive. It's so big—it covers so many people from all different places and backgrounds and beliefs and cultures. Any time you have such a massive group of people, there is no way to please everyone. So every time I'm seen with someone who isn't Hannah, I get a slew of comments about it. "Hannah's all natural!" is a big one. And that's true! Hannah is a naturally pretty girl. She's awesome. But every girl I date doesn't deserve to be stacked up against Hannah. I would never do that, and I hope that our culture learns to stop the judgment, too.

No matter who you are and no matter who you're talking about, saying something about someone's appearance is unproductive and can be really hurtful. We like to say we live in a culture where we no longer body shame, where we embrace everyone. But we don't.

As for me, I love bodies—all bodies. If you ask my buddies, they'll tell you—I love people of all shapes and sizes. I like tall girls and short girls and thin girls and curvy girls. I appreciate everyone. I see beauty in all people and all things. And I see everyone as worthy of respect.

To me, treating someone with respect goes beyond just doing the bare minimum. I want to make them feel like they *matter*. Because that's a feeling we all deserve.

I grew up loving R&B music and watching R&B videos. The cheesy way they would treat the girls in the videos—these huge romantic displays—is what I grew to idolize. So when it comes to dating, I like to treat. That's just my style. I would want my brothers to be that way, too. When I was younger and we went out, my mom gave us extra money to make sure we took care of our dates. That's just how we were taught. Now, if you get into a relationship with someone and you want to divide things one way or another, that's fine and that's your business. But when it comes to dating, one way I like to make my partner feel special is to treat her.

The same is true when it comes to sex. The fact that consent was such a big deal blew me over. That's, like, Respect 101. For me, treating someone right goes way beyond consent. I always make sure that any girl I'm with is in a place she wants to be. This especially means ensuring she's in a place where she's able to make those decisions—when someone is drunk, they can't make those decisions clearly, and that should never be taken advantage of. If one person wants to be in that moment and the other person doesn't, then it's not the right place and it's not the right time—for either of you.

What we see in the media, whether on TV or in the movies, is often an unhealthy and unrealistic representation of sex and consent.

We see the cool guy in the frat who brings a different girl up to his room every night. You hear stories about quarterbacks who went to a party and picked up a girl and went home with her. And on and on. It's easy to paint these pictures in your head, that this or that lifestyle is something to aspire to. But with experience, I have learned that's definitely not the guy you should emulate.

Before I had a serious relationship, sex was just sex. It was just fun. It was part of the party lifestyle that I had grown up around. But when I got into a real relationship, I saw how much more it can be and how much it can mean to the other person. I saw how much better sex can feel when it's part of a real connection. I understood that it wasn't a light matter at all.

Once I had a girlfriend, everything became so much better, because it was a shared experience with someone I really loved. To me, sex in the context of a relationship—consistent, consensual sex—was the best I've ever had, because we could communicate constantly. We knew what the other person liked, and we knew that we both wanted to be there, in that moment. I remember looking into my girlfriend's eyes and thinking, *I can't believe I get to be with this beautiful person*. That was the real connection I'd spent my whole life looking for.

Growing up, I never had anyone to tell me about sex. I didn't have an older brother. My dad and I didn't talk about that stuff. I never had anyone to have those conversations with. When it came to *real* sex, not just what I was seeing in R&B videos and on Pornhub (sorry, just being honest), I needed to figure things out for myself. Through a lot of trial and error, I eventually discovered that once you build an emotional bridge to somebody, that's where the real learning begins. The other day, I was joking with my friends that I didn't understand female anatomy until I had a girlfriend (I blame the public school system). But learning what she liked and what made her feel good is part of what made it exciting.

Sex is such an important part of dating. If you want to talk about a master class in consent, it's not just about whether someone wants to sleep with you. I think it goes deeper than that. I ask about *everything*—I don't leave anything up for question. And I think that's how it should be, at least until you're really comfortable with that person and know each other fully.

In that setting, you can never leave anything up for interpretation. So when I'm in bed, I ask about every little thing. *Can I take this off? Is this okay? What do you like?* Communication is everything. You need to talk things out. When I'm in bed with a girl, I am very vocal. I want to make sure that whatever we're doing is something that she's into. Something she enjoys and wants to do. The best sex happens when both parties are into it, not just because they're trying to please the other person. I want her to want to be there. There is no other way.

If a person is into something, and both parties have a conversation about it and think it's okay, that's one thing. But just because you see something happen in videos doesn't automatically mean it's on the table. If there's something you're interested in doing, have those conversations with the person and see if they're into it! If everyone is on the same page, then it's fine to move ahead.

Also, remember that there is no rush, and you should never feel pushed into anything. This one's a big one for me. I sometimes joke that I am most reserved around the girls I'm really, really into. I need to move at a pace I'm comfortable with. But I think that's okay. I've seen what sex does and doesn't mean to people, and I have learned to take it very seriously. I want to make sure it feels right for both of us before I dive in.

No woman should ever feel pressured. I may have a daughter one day, or a son, for that matter, and I don't want them to ever feel pressured—pressured to have sex, or to be or do anything that isn't true to who they are. I want them to have so much confidence in themselves that they know what's important and can stand up for what they want. The idea of having a daughter or son in this world is scary. If someone did something to hurt my kid, I wouldn't be able to live with myself. I hope that by the time I do become a parent, our culture's understanding of relationships, sex, and consent has evolved enough that I won't feel afraid.

I want the world to be a place where my daughter is free to speak her mind and make her own choices without judgment. I want her to be looked at as an equal, whether it's in the workplace or any-where else. I grew up in a household where my mom's job was to stay home and take care of the kids, though she went on to work as a real estate agent once we were old enough to take care of ourselves. She was the best mom, and that was right for her. But that's not right for everybody. I don't believe there are any "shoulds" in this world—I don't believe that women or men belong in any specific place, doing any specific thing. So when it comes to her life's work, I want my daughter to choose whatever is best for her and not feel swayed by others' opinions. When it comes to consent and sex and relation-ships, I want her opinion to matter just as much as the person she's with. I want her to always feel empowered enough to speak her mind.

I definitely believe that we speak things into existence. When you say something, you give it power. To that end, I know someone with two daughters. From the time they were little kids, my friend would always talk about them, saying that one daughter was going to grow up to be a doctor and the other daughter was going to grow up to get pregnant by the time she was sixteen. Well, guess what? They both went on to do exactly what everyone said about them.

I'm not yet a parent, so I fully admit that in this arena, I have no experience. But based on my own observations, it's clear to me that we need to be mindful of how we speak to our kids—both the things we say to them and the things we say about them—because you speak that into existence. What you say may seem benign, but words matter, and especially those of a parent.

I didn't have many conversations about sex with my parents. Whether it was because they were uncomfortable speaking to me about it or just assumed that I would learn from school or friends, I don't know. But I never had the birds and the bees conversation. I just had the "If you touch her, I'll break your hand" conversation with my dad, which only goes so far. I had to learn as I went, which isn't always the best way.

Now, I see that it's my duty to have these conversations. Even if it's hard at first, it leaves us all much better off than before. And the more you do it, the easier it gets. Kids need to learn there can be consequences to their actions and that it is our duty to prevent and protect one another from experiencing trauma. We need to mentor kids, and we need to have the right conversations to ensure everyone feels empowered to make good decisions.

When it comes to our society, I can only hope that consent becomes normalized. I hope we can get to a point where consent isn't praised, because it's just the norm. I hope for a world where someone doesn't get a trophy for doing what everyone should be doing.

The lesson for all of us is: Don't be afraid to speak up. Don't be afraid to ask questions. Don't be afraid to say no. Don't be afraid to talk to your date, your kids, your partner, your friends about sex. And just as important in all of these conversations, make sure you listen. It's up to all of us to work together to create a world where everyone feels safe, comfortable, and respected. It's what we all deserve.

PSA FOR ALL MEN

One day recently, I was scrolling through Instagram when I saw that a friend had shared something from an account called Girls Against Oppression. In this particular post, they posed a seemingly simple question: "What would women do if men weren't on this Earth?" As I read all the responses, I was blown away.

The answers were varied, but they all had one thing in common: they talked about what I would describe as simple liberties. The most common answer was "take a walk" or "take a walk at night." Here's a small sampling of what people said:

Go for a hike—at night, alone, or with friends
Go camping or spend time alone in nature
Wear whatever they wanted
Go dancing
Go for a jog with headphones on

Implement lasting political change
Live without fear

It probably goes without saying, but these are not outlandish things to want. As a man, I've had the privilege of living a life where I've been able to do many of these things without ever giving them a second thought. I've been fortunate enough to wear whatever I choose, walk around late at night, and go solo camping without worrying. In fact, as I write this, I've done all of those things in the past couple of weeks.

As I read through everyone's words, a heavy feeling settled over me. These were such simple, simple desires—things all people should be able to do—and yet so many female-identifying people don't feel comfortable exercising them. This realization made me feel terrible. For one, I'd taken this privilege for granted for most of my life. But more important, it made me think of my female friends and the women I care about. I want them to feel free to do and say and wear whatever they want, whenever they want. I want them (and all women) to always feel comfortable and safe as they go about their lives. The fact that they don't was hard to accept. But just because it's hard to accept doesn't mean I can afford not to. I know now that my voice is needed to help initiate the change that makes this world a more equal place.

A little while later, I was talking to one of my female friends about this, to get her perspective. After she shared some of her own experiences, I asked her, "How does this change?" She said that an important step is for men to develop a greater awareness of these issues and to take actions to help women feel safe. The more I discussed these ideas with the women in my life, the more I discovered that there are lots of things women have been conditioned to notice. They are aware of who else is around them, especially at night. They are wary of empty subway platforms, parks, parking lots, or sidewalks that aren't well-lit. They have their keys out and ready before they get to their front door.

For all the men who have the privilege of going about our days without many of these concerns, it's on us to make this a better world for women. It's undeniable that as a society, we're doing a poor job of that. But how do we go about actually making it happen?

For starters, these conversations need to be had. I think it's great that women are bringing these issues into the national conversation, raising awareness about these injustices, and I applaud everyone who is using their voice to do so. But it's never the duty of any oppressed party to teach everyone else about it. Yes, it's okay to find the women in your life and talk to them about it. As with all things, it's always good to seek out different perspectives and to listen to what other people have to say. But, men, we can bring up these issues, too, especially with other men. Groups of guys can talk about these problems and also discuss solutions, even when women aren't around. It's on us to help make a difference.

Next, it's time we hold one another accountable. For men, if we're out and we see a woman being disrespected, we need to say something. This also means we have to look out for one another. If I'm on a subway platform at night and I see a woman on her own, I keep one eye out to make sure that she doesn't encounter any danger. If I'm at a bar and I see some dude sidle up to a woman, I stay aware of the situation, to make sure she isn't being harassed.

In a big, urban center like New York, there is often an unwritten rule about minding your own business. It's not uncommon to be approached or mugged or even assaulted while none of the people around you stop to ask if you're okay. But we need to put an end to that. I'm not saying to stick your nose in everybody's business, but if I see another human being in need, I am always going to do what I can to check in on them and help however I can.

Finally, as men, we need to be more aware of how we make the women around us feel. This includes the things we say, as well as the way we look at them and treat them. We have to extend this to *all* women—both the women we know and the women we don't know. It is never okay to catcall a woman, to touch a woman, to disrespect a woman. Sometimes these things feel so obvious that I can't believe I need to write them down, but they continue to happen, so clearly on some level the message isn't getting through.

Guys, it's not a woman's job to correct us, nor is it her job to teach us. It's our job to hold one another accountable. Let's do better. Let's keep going until we *all* have what every human being deserves—the right to simply exist.

The Real Tyler:

· ·

ACCORDING TO HIS BROTHER RYAN

*Tyler definitely had a big leap in maturity when he was in col-*lege. When he came back to Florida to go to FAU, that's when I really saw him grow into the guy he is now. He's a busy bee—he's always in motion, always doing things. He'll wake up early and work out, then start cleaning or fixing things around the house.

Tyler thinks he's a singer, but he's not. He sings in the shower and on car rides, and it's really bad. He can pull off dancing, but I'm still the better dancer. He also thinks he can cook better than me, but he can't. I don't think he's ever made a mistake. The only thing wrong with Tyler is that his farts smell really bad.

When I was in high school, Tyler became more of a father figure to me. There was this one time I'll never forget. It was my senior year of high school; I was playing football and recruiting wasn't going well, so I started doubting myself. One day, Tyler and I got into an argument about laundry. We were folding laundry, everyone was in a bad mood, and it all just blew up, the way it sometimes does with brothers. But then he said this thing that stuck with me to this day. He walked up to me, poked me really hard in my chest, and said, "I believed in you before you ever believed in yourself." He showed me that he supported me the whole time. Throughout my life, he's showed me that I had so much potential and I just needed to unleash myself and let it come to good use.

When you talk about Tyler's character, there's one thing that sticks out: he's a leader. He strives to inspire the people around him. He's been a really big part of my growth, and he helped me become the person I am today. Tyler always talks about the importance of going big. Because of him, I decided to go to FAU to pursue the biggest-time football that I could, and I'm having the time of my life.

For as long as I can remember, Tyler has always looked out for me. He's always made sure I have what I need for the game; he's always backed me with whatever I want to do. When he came back from the show, I thought he might be different, but he's still the same big brother.

With our mom's passing, he has been completely there for me. If I ever get sad, I know I can call him, even at two in the morning, and that he would get on FaceTime and talk me through everything, making sure that when I hung up the phone, I was in a calmer, better mental state than I was. He's always been that person I can talk to, now more than ever.

Tyler is super selfless. He's a you-before-me kinda guy. A lot of it comes from my mom. My mom was always someone who put other people first. She was a real estate agent, and for most agents, after you're done with your clients, they'll usually go their own way. But with my mom, her clients became her friends. Long after the transaction would be over, you'd find her picking weeds or mowing their lawn. I think my brother saw that and wanted to be someone who helped others, too. He finds satisfaction in helping others, which is really cool.

Tyler can see when someone's hurting or when something's wrong and will try to help the person get through that. After our mom passed, I started working out as therapy, as a way to help myself heal. Tyler saw that—how weight lifting was a way for me to feel better— and he said, "I'm going to give you the best, because I love you." We rebuilt the garage as a home gym so I could have my own safe space. He's always had my back. You know when people say, "Who are the people you want to have in your corner?" Tyler's that person. He's going to go to battle for you.

To me, Tyler's always been famous. In Jupiter, Florida, everyone always knew who he was. He was the quarterback. He was doing things around the town. His name was always known in a positive way. Now it's just on a bigger scale. It's not at all surprising that it happened; it's more just dumbfounding that this is real.

6

BEING GOOD, DOING GOOD,
FEELING GOOD

*How I Found Myself
(and My Selflessness)*

Back when I played football, we had this mantra: Whether you think you had a great practice or a bad practice, it's never as good or as bad as you thought it was. The truth is, you'll never see it for what it was until you stand back and watch the film.

Your ego can play tricks on you if you let it. It can lead you to think you're the best, and it can lead you to think you're the worst. It can make you afraid to take a chance or to make a mistake. And it can really do a number on your confidence.

There was a time, not that long ago, when I had absolutely no confidence in myself. When I got cut from the Ravens, not only was my self-esteem in the gutter, my identity was in crisis, too. I had no idea who I was. I felt like I had no purpose. For my whole life, I put so much work in, and for what? I still couldn't make it happen. I felt like a loser.

For me, the road to self-confidence was a slow one. I took it one day at a time—studying, getting my general contractor's license, taking my life in a new direction—and as I started to invest back in myself, little by little, my confidence grew. What I learned along the way was that confidence isn't just about a feeling; it's a decision. It's a direction. It's created by the small actions you take every day. Eventually, those little things add up to believing in yourself.

Creating good habits is a solid way to build your confidence. I learned this one from my dad. Around a decade ago, he went through a dark time. When the market crashed in 2008, he lost everything he had—his home, his money, his family—and tried to drown his sorrows by drinking. But eventually, he decided to pick himself up off the ground and get to work. It took a lot of rumbling and a lot of stumbling, but now he's having the best business year and the best chapter of his life he's ever had. How did he do it? For him, and for a lot of people, that journey to living confidently started by taking small steps.

More specifically, my dad started by making his bed every day. That's all. That one small task gave him the confidence to add on another small task, and another small task, and another small task, until eventually they started to add up to big changes. While you're developing new habits, keep in mind that it's okay to backslide sometimes. There might be days when you don't hit your goal, and that's okay. Try to do better tomorrow. We all have times when we mess up; that's part of the process. The important thing is that you keep going.

Any time you're trying something new, mistakes come with the territory. On my first job doing construction, I screwed up plenty. When you're building a house, you have to measure the openings to fit the windows. Well, I mismeasured them, and all the openings were two inches smaller than they were supposed to be. To try to fix it, I had to rent a concrete saw, which I had never used before. I had no idea what I was doing. There was a plug-in for a hose, which I ignored, so I turned on the saw, and the next thing I knew, I was shooting concrete straight up in the air. Meanwhile, I ended up covering everyone and everything in concrete soot, which meant other people couldn't do their jobs. By the end of the day, everyone working around me got angry and left. Was it my proudest moment? No. Was it the end of the world? Also no. But I owned up to my mistakes that day and worked with my supervisor to learn the skills I needed to fix them. You better believe that the next time I needed to use those tools, I had learned the proper way and was prepared to do my job.

My dad likes to say, "You learn from your mistakes when they're either painful or expensive." And I've had plenty of both. But I've found that when you use them as learning experiences and don't dwell on them for too long, they don't have to feel like a big deal. The first time you try something, it's okay not to feel confident. In fact, the first time you do any new thing, I think it's okay to feel proud of yourself just for trying.

In my own life, I like to make lists to keep myself accountable. I have three notebooks I write everything down in—one for my goals, one for my ideas, and one for my to-do lists. I also keep a list on my calendar, where I write down everything I need to do—making calls, going over bills, doing errands. Before I go to bed, I make a list for the next day, so that when I wake up, I know exactly what I need to take care of. That way I won't waste any time trying to get organized; I can hit the ground running.

I love to listen to motivational speakers, and Eric Thomas and Inky

Johnson are my guys right now. ET talks about waking up and attacking your to-do list every day. He says you need to be like a sniper. Take just one shot and get it done. If you're not focused, you wind up all over the place, and at the end of the day, you will have wasted all this time and still won't have accomplished what you wanted to.

I also keep a running list of my ideas. You always think you'll remember things, but then you don't. So whenever something pops into my head, I write it down so it isn't lost.

Making lists is such a simple thing, but doing so has completely changed my life. It's like applying my mantra of "one step at a time" to what I do every day. Goals are only as good as the milestones you set beneath them. When you set a goal—any goal, whether it's running a marathon or cleaning your house—it's important to break it down into different benchmarks along the way. You don't need to try to complete the whole journey; that can be overwhelming. Instead, create a detailed log of all the steps you need to take in order to get there, and then attack them one by one. That's another reason I love making lists—you can check things off as you accomplish them, which feels really good.

When it comes to attacking your day, Eric Thomas has another one I love. He says, in essence, that he starts his day at 4:00 a.m. and works for five hours before the genius ever gets to the office. You may not be as smart or as talented at something as the person next to you, but you can always work twice as hard. And oftentimes, that's enough to carry you where you want to go.

I've tried a bunch of things in my life, and some have definitely gone better than others. But what I've learned is that with hard work and belief, you can be whatever you want. If I really want to be a designer, I can be. Will I be Louis Vuitton? No. Will I be good at it right away? Definitely not. But with practice and a lot of work, you can figure anything out. If something lights you up and you find you have a real passion for it, you can listen and learn from others. And if you combine that with effort, anything is possible.

Once you've mastered creating small habits, the next step is to anchor them in a disciplined lifestyle. One of my favorite fitness coaches, Alex Toussaint, always says, "Discipline will carry you when motivation won't." He tells this story about when he was first starting out. He hadn't yet made a name for himself and was teaching cycling classes for maybe five or ten people. But his mentor always told him, "Creating enthusiasm isn't about how you make people feel in a crowded room; it's how *you* create that kind of energy, even when you're all alone. When there's no one else in the room, how do you create that kind of momentum and excitement for yourself?" He kept at it, and eventually the consistency paid off. Now he'll teach a virtual class for seventy-five thousand people at a time. It's all about showing up and putting the right energy into it, day after day. Discipline will get you through those days when motivation just isn't showing up.

Whenever I'm feeling down or having trouble connecting to my purpose, I find that looking outside myself is often the answer. When you get caught up in your own mind, you can spiral. You can easily lose touch with reality and what's really important. But when you do something to help someone else, it lifts your spirit like nothing else.

My favorite saying is "Through love, serve one another." I don't even remember where or how I found it, but it stuck with me immediately, because it's so simple and to the point. If you're going to do something, do it with love. Don't do it with any other expectations. Don't do it because you want anything in return; just do it out of love. That will bring you happiness, whether you're struggling to find it or not. For me, serving other people, helping them out, is what excites me. Whenever I'm upset about something, I say, "I have to go help people." That always gets me out of my head and picks me up at the same time.

I learned that from my mom, who was the ultimate servant. She took care of me, my brothers, my teammates—anyone who walked in to our home. Everyone who came through that door, no matter who they were, would find food on the table. She would help my friends and teammates, even if I wasn't home. She was just that kind of person. My mom always found a way to help the community, too. In our town, she ran an organization to help underprivileged kids, which she built from the ground up. She wanted everyone to be their best, to get to the top of their potential. I think she got more out of seeing other people happy, and she passed that down to my brothers and me.

Like I mentioned, one of my favorite questions to ask people is "What would you do if a dollar never mattered?" because it shows you what their purpose really is. If someone were to turn that question around on me, I would say that I would be a football coach and help kids get to college. That's been my dream ever since I was in high school, but not for the reason you might expect.

Growing up, I was best friends with this kid, James. We first met in fifth grade, on the travel basketball team. We were like a one-two punch—the two biggest kids in our age group in Florida, because we grew before everyone else did. James and I dominated at sports. Our team won the state championship when we were in ninth grade, when we were the only two freshmen to make varsity. We always trained together, and I remember the two of us sneaking off into the locker room to take naps before our games. Our freshman and soph-omore years, all these college coaches came to see me and James. He was six two, 240 pounds, and could bench 400 pounds—as a fifteen-year-old kid. He was smart, too; he had everything going for him. We were the two rising stars, and it seemed inevitable that our fu-tures would be tied together.

James had four brothers, and his mom worked full-time and took care of them all. His dad lived in town, but he was never really a part of James's life. All along, James always tried to be the big dog—he was big, he knew he was big, and he wanted everyone to know it. He would hang out with the older kids and act tough, and when we were in high school, he started going down the wrong path. "Stay with me," I told him. "Stay by me, and we'll be fine. We'll get through this together." But he went on a different road, one I didn't want to follow him down.

One of his brothers was on the team with us, and he could be trouble. One day our sophomore year, we were getting blown out in a football game, and everyone was pissed. His brother wasn't getting to play, and he said, "We need to walk off." The coach was furious, and James was stuck in the middle.

The coach said, "If you leave, you're done."

But when his brother walked off the field, James followed behind him. The coach kept his word and kicked them off the team.

It was all downhill after that.

James got his girlfriend pregnant at sixteen. From that point for-ward, he was faced with all these grown-up decisions that he wasn't fully capable of making at that age. There were outside influences at play, and he was really young and impressionable. He got involved in some tough things, which got him in trouble and eventually landed him in prison. When I went away to college, James got shot. Thankfully, he was okay—we're still friends, and we catch up when we can. But he could have been so much more. He had so much potential; he could probably be playing in the NFL right now. He had all the talent and all the ability to succeed in this world. But when we were fifteen, he lived in a tough area without much guidance, and I feel like our coach, someone who could have been a real mentor to him, let him down. James was forced to make mature decisions at too young of an age.

I've thought about that moment, when he walked off the field and the coach just let him, a lot over the years. This was a special, talented kid with a big heart. He was a kid who had the whole world in front of him, and in that critical moment, the coach just let him go. There were a lot of influences at play there, but I believe that our coach failed him. If that had been me, I would have grabbed on to him and not let him go. I would have told him, "You can't go. We need you here. You've gotta stay." I think that with some kids, you need to find a way to be there for them, to hang on to them and tell them to keep going. It's tough, but some kids just haven't had someone grab on to them before. God knows that when I was younger, I didn't always make the right choices or do the right things, but I had a dad who wouldn't have let me leave that game. He would have told me to sit my ass back down on the bench and be ready to play. That kind of influence wasn't around for James, but of course that wasn't his fault. And yet he was the one who had to suffer the consequences.

I think about that all the time, about the things that some kids get because of privilege and the things other kids miss out on. Ever since I saw what happened to James, I've thought: *I want to do what that coach didn't do.* And that's what I plan to do one day. I know how much college changed my life and the lives of people around me, and I want to help other kids to have that experience. I want to hold tight to the kids who need somebody to help guide them.

What brings me joy is seeing the light switch that goes off in kids' heads, seeing the pride they feel when they work at something and then see their efforts pay off. There's nothing better than when other people have that proud moment when they suddenly say, "Oh shit, I can do this." So many coaches have made a difference in my life— I've quoted a lot of them throughout this book, because their words and their lessons had an effect on me—and one day I want to do the same for other kids.

These days, one of my favorite ways to spend time is through ABC Food Tours, where I get to give back and really enjoy myself while I'm doing it. ABC Food Tours is something my friend Matt James started. One day, Matt was taking a group of people out to eat at his favorite spot, Bobwhite in the East Village, and these kids were outside the restaurant, making fun of him for his short shorts. He asked them, "Have you ever been to Bobwhite?" They hadn't. So he went to their school principal the next day and was like, "You don't know me from Adam, but I'd love to take these kids on a food tour." And the school let him. As it turned out, giving tours to kids was a ton of fun, so we decided to keep on going. The program has been evolving ever since, and it has grown so much. Just the other day, we donated four thousand meals ($72,000 worth of food) to one of the public schools on Manhattan's Lower East Side.

It's amazing giving kids an experiential tour of their own city, taking them places and having them try all these foods they may not otherwise get to experience. We also bring different people on the tours to help us host it, so they can talk to kids about their careers and help expose them to different opportunities. When we ask the kids about what jobs they might want when they grow up, we always get the same answers: football player, basketball player, police officer, rapper, or YouTube star. So we try to open up their eyes to different avenues that could also be available to them in the future.

We dance through the city—we play music on a Bluetooth speaker, and the kids jam and have fun. We ask them questions, get them thinking. We like to believe we're serving those kids, but we know we're also learning so much from them—from their energy and from their stories. I get to hang out and be a kid again. Those are the most exciting days of the week.

One day, a bunch of us had just finished doing the Electric Slide in Tompkins Square Park, and I sat down on a bench with this little kid. The two of us sat there, watching skateboarders, eating pizza, and he said, "This is the best day I've ever had." My heart just melted. Until that point, I hadn't realized the impact we were having on these kids.

Another time, one kid was wearing cargo shorts, and Matt and I noticed his pockets were full. While the rest of the kids were eating, he said he wasn't really hungry, but he wrapped up his sandwich and his snacks and packed them away, for his mom and his sister. He told us he wasn't going to eat his lunch so that his family could eat instead. Of course, we got him some extra food so he could take it home. But these stories are reminders that you never know what someone has going on behind the scenes. ABC Food Tours has really opened my eyes. One, to what really matters. And two, that there are problems so much bigger than my own that need my attention.

• • • • •

Everything is connected. The better I can make others feel, the better I feel.

For a lot of people, faith is another avenue to help feel grounded, and following any religion is a way that people find their purpose. Personally, I'm a Christian and I believe in God, but I also know I don't always walk the straightest, most faithful line. Depending on where I am in my life, the path can be pretty loosey-goosey. But I've gotten much better as I've gotten older. I like to think that's a result of growth and learning from my past mistakes.

When my mom passed, it really opened my eyes to spirituality. I had always had questions about the meaning of life, but her passing really made me think. If there's no afterlife, if there's no greater why beyond this, then what's the point? I hope that I'll get to see her again one day. In the meantime, no matter what happens, it made me want to live a better life. And that's what I'm trying to do, day by day—make Momma proud.

BUILD YOUR TEAM:
LESSONS FROM MY MENTORS

· ·

If there's one thing I've learned over the years, it's that it's important to surround yourself with people who help you grow. For those of us who don't come from ideal circumstances—and really, who does?—you can find role models and inspiration elsewhere. From friends and family to mentors and gurus, I've learned so much by connecting with people I admire.

Here are some of the most important things I've learned from my mentors, as well as ways you can find some mentors of your own . . .

BUILD YOUR TEAM

For me, having a mentor isn't just about having one guru to teach me all the things. Oftentimes, successful people have a whole team behind them, made up of agents, managers, publicists, assistants. They recognize that surrounding themselves with people who are good at different things ultimately makes them better. Companies will often have a board of directors to help guide the business. I think, no matter who you are or where it is you want to go in life, everyone can benefit from making their own personal board of directors.

Ideally, you want to have different people fill different roles. You want someone who's a cheerleader, someone who tells it to you straight, someone who lifts you up and inspires you, someone who pushes you to be better, someone to call you out when you're not being the best you can be. They can be people whose words really move you, or they can be people who lead by example. Some of them can be people you know in real life, while some of them can be people you've never met before.

Some people might be better at talking about relationships, while another person might only focus on business. As you grow and change, your board of directors can change, too.

FIND WHAT RESONATES

I've been blessed to have a bunch of mentors in my life who have really helped me. Some of them I know personally, and some of them I don't. As I've said, my parents weren't the healthiest role models when it came to relationships and communication. But even if you're lucky enough to come from a family full of role models, it can be helpful to widen your circle to get different perspectives and world views.

Sometimes, when you get a piece of advice from your family, you don't necessarily hear it because it's coming from them. (You know what I'm talking about.) But when you hear the exact same idea from someone else you look up to—maybe it's a friend who's a little older, or a boss or a coach or even a celebrity—you listen. People have different ways of framing things. You can hear the same lesson forty different ways, but you have to find the person who's going to put it in a way that really hits home for you.

LEARN BY OBSERVING

I've had role models who didn't even know they were role models. Remember my roommate from Wake Forest? He was the angel when I was the devil. He was responsible when it came to both school and football, and he won National Student-Athlete of the Year. He was the greatest kid ever. I always admired his actions, yet in the moment, I made fun of him for them. But when things didn't work out for me and I started looking in the mirror, he's who I thought of as an example of someone I wanted to be like. I never told him he was my role model, and he'll never know how much his example helped me to become a better person (unless he reads this book). Secret role models can be just as effective as any other.

Another secret role model was my teammate Aziz, who was my college locker room buddy at Florida Atlantic University. His work ethic was second to none. After our games, we would fly home at 4:00 a.m., and he would go straight to the film rooms while all of us went to sleep. He's Muslim, and during Ramadan he would fast. Even though he couldn't eat all day, he would still do two practices a day and bring his all out on the field. I really admired his commitment to both his faith and his sport. He's now playing for the 49ers, and he put himself in that position by always showing up and doing what he needed to do. Seeing how hard he worked, and continues to work, inspires me to be better.

FIND SIMILARITIES

Some of the people on my board of directors are very similar to me—similar personalities, similar life experiences, similar challenges—and that's helpful because there is a natural understanding between us. It's really valuable to feel like someone knows where you're coming from.

I didn't grow up with an older brother, but I have four honorary older brothers I can call on: Robb, Drew, Alex, and Paul. The latter three are actual brothers, who grew up down the street from me. They're all around a decade older than I am, and in a way, they raised me. I would always be over there, asking to play basketball with them, trying to be more like them. Drew lives in New York now, and we still play in a basketball league together. Their opinions matter so much to me.

I met Robb when I was in high school, and the circumstance of our meeting was pretty serendipitous. Okay, stay with me here: My uncle once dated a lady named Amy. They broke up, but we all loved Amy so much that we stayed friends and continued to see her. Soon after, Amy started dating this guy named Wiley, whose name is perfect for him, because he's the wiliest person you'll ever meet. He and my dad are good friends—they hunt, they fish, they're crazy. Wiley's my kind of people.

One day during my junior year, I went out to lunch with my best friend and our two moms. We were talking about college and about football, minding our own business, when some guy sitting near us asked me, "Are you one of the Cameron boys?" He heard me talking and figured out who I was.

He extended his hand. "I'm Robb."

Robb is Wiley's cousin. (Still with me?) Just the day before, Wiley told him how he needed to meet the Camerons. "They're just like us," he said. "They love fishing and getting into trouble and having fun." And then, just like that, I appeared in front of him. Our friendship was meant to be. From that point on, Robb became like a big brother I never had. I have always been able to ask him questions and get his take on things, which was really valuable to me. I had never had someone around like that.

As I got to know him, I discovered that he and I had a lot in common. When Robb was younger, he played college basketball, but just like me, he was often his own worst enemy. He was a knucklehead who spent his college years partying and ultimately got in his own way. After college, he kept living the wild life, making good money and partying with all the athletes and all the girls. He has the craziest stories about being a rebel.

Then one day, he met a girl, Anna, who was really good for him. He knew she was his perfect match, and even though it took him a while to settle down, to break the habits of his party days, he knew he couldn't let her get away.

Now, they're married, they have two kids, and they take on the world together.

Role models can lead by voice or they can lead by action. Even though Robb does not shut up—seriously, he can talk forever—in my eyes, he does a lot of leading by action. One of the best things for me has been seeing the relationship he has with Anna. They're two people who both have their own goals and dreams—she's an actress, and he loves real estate. They support each other's passions, and they go for what they want, separately and together.

Robb and Anna have so much love and respect for each other; they're like their own little team. I also really admire the way they handle their kids and extended family. Robb is that dad who gets to spend a lot of time with his kids and is super involved in their lives. Through Robb, I can see firsthand the sort of healthy relationship model I didn't always have growing up. To me, what they have is the dream.

INCLUDE YOUR FRIENDS

My best friends Mollie, Katie, and Matt are part of my board of directors, too. Any time I need guidance, I can trust that they always have my best interest at heart. It's helpful to have people in your life whom you can call on for a quick survey. I'm always calling one or another of them and asking, "Hey, what do you think of this?" I also look up to Mollie because I really admire the relationship she has with her boyfriend. I like being around them because it's helpful to see how they lead by example (plus, he's a really good chef).

LOOK FURTHER AFIELD

When it comes to finding mentors, don't discount people you don't know in real life. If someone says something that resonates with you—whether it's on TV or a podcast or in an article or on social media—and you find them inspiring, then add them to your personal board of directors. A lot of the coaches and motivational speakers I follow are people I found randomly. I believe that everything comes to me for a reason, with the advice or wisdom I need at that time.

I first discovered Eric Thomas (also known as ET, the Hip Hop Preacher) through a viral video. It was about a kid playing football at East Carolina University, but the background audio was Eric

Thomas speaking. He told a story about this young businessman who meets a guru. The guru tells him to meet him at the beach. When he arrives, the guru tells him to get in the water. The kid's like, "Get in the water? What does that have to do with business?" but he does as he's told. The guru keeps telling him to go deeper and deeper, until he reaches the point where he can't stand anymore. Then, the guru shoves him down, holding his head under the water.

After some time, finally, the guru lets him up for air. At this point, the kid is pissed.

"Do you want to kill me?" he asks.

The guru tells him, "When you want to succeed as bad as you want to breathe, then you'll be successful."

That story really stuck with me. It's an extreme example, of course, and I do not condone attempted drowning in the pursuit of business acumen, but sometimes you need to be extreme to get the point across.

I found Inky Johnson, another mentor I follow, when he came to speak at FAU. I wasn't there for his speech, but after I heard about it, I went and looked him up. He has such a singular story. He came from nothing. He had a big family, but when he was growing up, they only had two bedrooms, so they would rotate who got to sleep in a bed. Every three days or so, he would sleep in a bed, and the rest of the time, he slept on the floor.

When he got older, everyone around him wanted to go to this swanky, sports-focused high school, where every football player who came out of there was a five-star recruit. But Inky wanted to do it his own way. He'd rather go to a school where no one had ever done that before, so he could achieve that goal on his own. And that was exactly what he did. He was getting attention from colleges and wound up going to the University of Tennessee. While at Tennessee, he had a great athletic career and was projected to be a first-round draft pick in the NFL. But then, during his senior year, he went to make a tackle that went terribly wrong. His injury paralyzed his right arm. Just like that, his football career was over. For a lot of people, that might have derailed their entire lives, but he never quit. He went on to become a motivational speaker, where he talks about the importance of never giving up.

As soon as I heard what he had to say, I really connected with him, because I've come to believe that quitting and self-doubt—all those negative things that derail you from going after your goals—are a cancer. One quote of his really speaks to me: "People get upset not because of the adversity they face but because adversity reveals who they truly are." When I got kicked off the team at Wake Forest, the hardest part was that it made me confront who I was and the role I played in making that happen. Adversity forces you to be accountable.

Inky talks a lot about how, if you quit, you set an example for your kids and future generations, and it perpetuates the cycle. This is true even if you don't have kids. If you give up, you're setting a pattern in motion, and it trickles down to everyone who depends on you. I love that mentality, and it's something I always keep in mind. I don't just need to work hard for myself. If I keep messing up, I let my brothers down, I let my agents down, I let the rest of my family down. I do what I do to help put other people in better positions. Our success is tied to one another's.

To be honest, though, I still battle with this all the time. I have moments when I get frustrated and say to myself, *If this doesn't work out, I'll just give up and go coach football.* I do dream of coaching football one day, but there are a lot of other things I want to accomplish in the meantime. Sometimes it feels like it would be so easy to just live easy and call it life, but I don't want to do that. I don't want to live with regret for what might have been if only I had faith in myself.

RENT WHAT YOU DON'T YET OWN

Everyone's heard that phrase *Fake it 'til you make it.* But like with any platitude, it's such a classic piece of advice because it works. Along those same lines, one of my favorite pieces of Inky Johnson wisdom is that if you can't believe in yourself just yet, you can rent someone else's belief until you're strong enough to develop your own.

For a long time, I didn't have any self-confidence. The truth is, when I decided to be more like my roommate, Ryan, I didn't just try to act more like him. I essentially rented Ryan's belief in himself. Every step of the way, I tried to envision what Ryan would do—and also how Ryan would *feel.* Eventually, that started to wear off on me. When I saw I could do it myself, I started to develop my own self-confidence, but I had to fake it until I got there.

As the football coach Pete Carroll would say, "If you don't feel enthusiastic, then fake it." Sometimes you're exhausted or overwhelmed or feel like you can't bring it. On those days, you just have to pretend. That false bravado will eventually turn real one day, if you keep on pushing it out there.

GET UNCOMFORTABLE

Back in my football days, I had this one coach, Charlie Partridge, who was always telling us we needed to get out of our comfort zone.

When we were training, he would tell us stories about how to raise the threshold of our comfort zones. One of his favorites was about raising the temperature of the room—from seventy-five to seventy-eight to eighty degrees. The idea was that every time you get used to it, you're supposed to raise the temperature again. Those stories were his way of pushing us to get better, and better, and better.

Sometimes it can be tempting to fall into the same old routines. Trying a new thing, especially if it's something you're afraid of, can feel disorienting. Also, the first time you try any new thing, there's a pretty good chance you're going to suck at it. That's okay. It comes with the territory. It's not always fun, but you grow so much from making yourself uncomfortable. Once you get to a new comfort level, try something new and make your comfort level grow again.

Speaking of comfort levels, it reminds me of my first time shooting for the show *Barkitecture*. If you aren't familiar, I hosted a show where we went to celebrities' homes and made these really elaborate doghouses for their dogs. This was my first time working on a project like this, so it was an entirely new experience for me. I'm a pretty reserved, laid-back person, especially around new people. When we arrived at one of the homes, the person was, shall we say, not welcoming. Although they very clearly knew we were coming, they acted confused and almost annoyed as to who I was and why I was there. And yet, once the cameras started rolling, it was a totally different story. They were so friendly and over-the-top, you'd have thought they were an entirely different person.

When that happened, my first instinct was to say, "Fuck this." It left a bad taste in my mouth when it came to all things involving Hollywood, and all of a sudden I was questioning a career path in entertainment. I was uncomfortable. This wasn't the world I was used to, and I was out of my element. But I had to come to terms with the fact that I wasn't going to jell with everyone in this world. That's what comes along with a job in the entertainment industry.

Not everything you do, or everyone you work with, will feel like a natural fit, especially not at first. As I started pushing myself out of my comfort zone, I relaxed and was able to be myself despite the challenges of my surroundings. Now, when I step in front of a camera, I can bring 50 percent more energy than I did before, because I've expanded my comfort zone. Every time, I try to push that number higher.

This was just as true back when I was getting my general contractor's license. I remember on the first day of class, I left that classroom so distraught. I felt screwed. Everything was so foreign to me—there were so many terms I had never even heard before. It really seemed like there was no way in hell I was going to pull that one off. But as I put one foot in front of the other, my understanding grew. So did my comfort zone.

When it comes to your comfort level, you can work on expanding that slowly. It all comes back to the basic mantra of breaking down your journey into small parts. Just focus on one good thing, then the next good thing, then the next good thing.

KNOW YOUR BLIND SPOTS

There's wisdom in knowing your strengths and weaknesses. I find that the people I naturally admire are often people who are strong at whatever I'm weak at. Right now, I feel weakest when it comes to business. I have a guy who helps with my taxes, and sometimes I have to call him and say, "I don't know what the hell you're talking about!" When it comes to financial literacy and basic everyday business skills like how to file your taxes, I'm better than I used to be, but I still have a lot to learn. But it's a good thing I recognize that, because it allows me to consult and rely on people who have those skills.

It's important to be aware of your strengths and to know your areas for improvement. (They're not even necessarily your weak spots, because more than likely, they're just areas where you don't have a lot of experience and need some time to learn.) Once you know what you don't know, then you can find people who are strong in that area to help you out.

FIND WHAT WORKS FOR YOU

It can be helpful to know your communication style and what works well for you. Do you need things sugarcoated, or do you like when someone tells it like it is? Do you learn better from people who have a tough-love approach? You might want to build your team with different people with different styles for different occasions, and that works, too!

For me, I've discovered I am often better at communicating when it comes to having conversations with people who are open, enthusiastic, and emotionally vulnerable. Someone who naturally exhibits those things helps to bring out the same qualities in me. When I talk to my agents, for example, I can ask them questions and I don't feel like I have to be big or strong or macho. I don't have to pretend to have all the answers or to be anyone I'm not. I appreciate that they're straight shooters who share their honest opinions and experiences with me. That communication style helps take the ego out of the conversation, so I can just let it go and be real and be loose. They help me out with my shit, they tell it like it is, and they always look out for me, and I appreciate it.

CHOOSE WISELY

Just as important as finding people you can learn from is finding people you can trust. If you're going to let someone onto your board of directors, you want to be sure they have your best interests in mind. Before I let someone into my inner circle, I'm careful about making completely sure they're someone I can trust. (If I meet someone and they start talking about partnering together right off the bat, or they show me they have ulterior motives, I'm out.)

When you find good people who have your back, there's nothing better. This one agent of mine has been the biggest blessing. She's also from South Florida, and she gets the kind of person I am. (Florida people are different people. We're like our own wild species! The internet will confirm. I think it's because Florida has all the extremes—extreme weather, extreme temperatures—and it just produces extreme people.) My agent is someone I know I can always talk to, about business but also about life. She helped me with my transition to moving to New York. When my mom passed away, she was there for me. I know she always has my back, on a personal level and on a business level. She's the kind of person you want to represent you.

LISTEN TO THOSE WHO CAME BEFORE

I've learned from personal experience that it can be really helpful to talk to people who have gone places before you or who have had similar jobs, relationships, or lifestyles to ones you hope to have.

That way, you'll get the chance to learn about experiences before you even get to them. It's almost like seeking out a travel guide for life.

I told my friend Matt, "Before you go on *The Bachelor*, you should talk to some of the previous bachelors. Seek out the guys who have been in those shoes before and see what stories and advice they have for you. You may not agree with them, and you may have a completely different experience, and that's okay. But I'm sure there will be instances and moments in time when you'll say, 'Ohhh, *that's* what he was talking about.'"

The same is true for anyone. If you're interested in going to a new school or working at a certain company or moving to a new town, seek out people who have gone to that school or worked for that company or lived in that town and see if they're willing to talk to you about it.

PUT ON YOUR BLINDERS

Whatever you do, focus on your own journey. Look at the road ahead of you, and nowhere else. If you look to the side and try to see what someone else has or what they're working on, it's just going to derail you from your path.

Everyone is on their own time clock. Whatever it is you're after—school, a job, love, a family—there is no one timeline of when those things are "supposed" to happen or how they're "supposed" to be. If you look around, it's easy to get tripped up seeing what other people have and comparing yourself. Social media especially causes so many people to struggle with this.

I'll catch myself saying things like, "If this doesn't work out in two years . . ." followed by some defeatist backup plan. Then I'll stop myself and think: *What am I doing? I'm giving up on something before I even get started because I think it needs to happen in a certain way? Bro, you're better than that.*

You have plan A. Don't settle for anything less. And be patient as you work toward it.

You have to learn to run your race just like a horse with blinders on. Comparing yourself to other people is a way to make yourself anxious and unhappy, creating all this pressure around what you think you should have. Really focus on yourself and your goals and dreams. Don't worry about some imaginary clock of success or romance. Just focus on everything you can do in the meantime to help get yourself on the best path possible for you. Remember, success is what happens when opportunity meets preparedness. Your time will come. And when it does, you'll be prepared.

ASK FOR BACKUP

There's nothing wrong with saying, "I'm gonna do it my way." But sometimes—speaking from personal experience here—you might try to do something alone and you'll see your way fail. For a long time, I was that stubborn person who was too macho and had too much pride to ask for help. But I've learned, the more I ask—for advice, for feedback, for assistance—the more I grow. The more I humble myself, too.

If asking is uncomfortable, start small. You can even beat around the bush a little bit. Do whatever it takes to open up those doors and get the backup you need. Keep in mind that people like to help. It makes them feel good, too. If you're in over your head, or you're confused about something, or you don't know the next step to take, call your board of directors.

Remember, no one knows everything. A lot of people mess up in life because they want to believe they know everything (or at least pretend like they do), but you can get further with a team. Don't block your blessings by being afraid to have a guru. Don't be too stubborn to ask for help or call on your board of directors when you need them. Just like successful companies have advisors, successful people have them, too.

7

DATING DOS AND DON'TS

Red Flags and Green Lights

Before we talk about dating other people, let's talk about you.

As cliché as it sounds, when people say, "You need to love yourself before you can love another person," it's 100 percent true. You have to love who you are and what you're doing with your life in order to give real love to someone else. I wish I could tell you that I've found a magic shortcut, but unfortunately, there is no way around this hard work.

Back when I was dating Mariah, I didn't love myself. I wasn't yet secure in who I was. When we first got together, I loved where my life was going—getting my MBA, playing football, eventually trying to go pro. But I hadn't built an identity outside of those things. When all those dreams fell apart, I fell apart. And along the way, I didn't give back what she gave me. I wasn't able to offer her the love and respect and attention she deserved. That was part of my journey of learning and growing; I was still finding myself. But I learned you need to check yourself *before* putting yourself out there. Otherwise somebody's going to get hurt. I still feel regret that I hurt Mariah in this way.

It's easy to feel that pressure to want to be with somebody. Our society makes it seem like you need to have a partner, or like you need to settle down by a certain age. But here's the truth: being alone is better than settling for less than you deserve. You can't waste your life with people who don't enhance it. Plus, being on your own can be a great thing. It allows you to work on yourself and figure out what you really want. When you take some time to be alone, it gives you the space to be reflective. It lets you figure out what's really important. Being intentional benefits everybody.

Some of my greatest growing moments happened when I was by myself. I have the best realizations when I'm working out alone or winding down at the end of the night. Those are the moments when I'm just contemplating, thinking about what I've gone through this past year and all the places I've been. That's also when I become aware of my fears, my bad patterns, and the things I run away from.

I get a lot of comments from people who say my intentions have changed since being on the show: "You said you wanted to build a future with Hannah, but now that you're off the show, you're not looking for that anymore." That's not true. I still want to find the right person and settle down. But now that I'm off the show, my life looks completely different than it did before, and so I'm doing the smart thing and reassessing my goals.

As I write this, I know I'm in a place where I'm actually not ready to be dating. I want to find the right person for me, and I think I've done the work to better understand how to be a good partner. But a lot has happened over the past year. A lot has changed. I'm still struggling with the loss of my mother, and I'm still feeling hurt. I don't want to get into a new relationship until I've processed those feelings, because I don't want to project that onto someone else. Hurt people hurt others, and I'd rather be alone than in a place where I could hurt someone.

For me, choosing not to date is a conscious decision. Right now, I'm working on making myself whole again. I'm focusing on work and healing and doing the things that make me happy, and hopefully I'll find someone along the way who wants to do those things with me. But until I find that, I'm not pushing it.

The point is, you don't need to do what anyone else, including society, tells you to. You don't need to be married with kids and a house by the time you're thirty (or ever). You can do that if it works for you, but it's not necessary. You can make your own decisions, on your own timetable, based on what's best for your life.

It's also important to look at your past and come to terms with it. See where maybe you messed up or what you were missing. Take accountability for your role in failed relationships, and then move forward. Everything from your past—good and bad—can help you learn a lesson.

For me, my biggest shifts happened after thinking about what went wrong in my prior relationships—both romantic relationships with Mariah and Hannah, and also my relationship with my mom. I look back and wish I had told my mom that I loved her more. When I think back to my last phone call with her, she was pissed at me, and we didn't say we loved each other. I had no idea I would never get the chance to tell her that again. If I didn't stop and look that experience in the eye, it might make me shut down and not show love to someone else. It might make me fearful of opening up in the future. But I want to do the opposite. I can have a hard time expressing my emotions. It's still hard for me to tell my brothers I love them. But I do, because I never want to make that mistake again.

If you don't stop and examine your past, you'll just repeat your patterns. We all have that friend who is in the same bad relationship over and over again, or who always chooses the wrong people. If this sounds like you, really stop and examine the choices you've made so you don't fall into those same traps again.

Ask yourself: Where am I going? What am I doing? What am I looking for in a relationship? What do I have to offer someone right now? Have those hard relationship conversations *with yourself*, because you need to know the answers before you can have them with someone else. That's what will give you clarity. If you find you don't like some of the answers, that's okay. What are you going to do to make it different? What are you going to change?

Before you're ready for a relationship, the goal is to get to a place where you feel like you have your shit together. I'm not saying everything needs to be perfect, because of course you're going to be working toward different things for your entire life. But you want to work on yourself enough so that you're secure in who you are.

I understand what it's like to crave being with someone. But once you learn to love being alone, that's when you discover what really makes you happy. Once you recognize that you don't need someone else to make you feel whole, you'll be in a place where you can make the best choices possible. Then the goal will be to find someone who just adds to that happiness. That last part goes for all relationships—dating, friendships, even business relationships. You want to build something you're proud of, and then find people who make it even better. The right partner is someone who complements and enhances what you already have going on.

Dating in the real world is obviously totally different than dating on *The Bachelorette*. They put you in the craziest predicaments, surrounded by the most beautiful scenery, and you do all these amazing things on a super-accelerated timeline. For weeks, you see no other women, and you look past anything that could possibly be a red flag and just keep going, all in the hopes that you'll get engaged in just a few months.

In the real world, there's a whole different set of rules. Timetables are different. People play games. Red flags are real and worth paying attention to. Sometimes love hits you in the face, and other times it's not so obvious. Shit can be complicated. I'm no expert, but I've learned a lot through my own experiences, both when I was right and when I wasn't. So, if you're in a place where you feel ready to get out there in the dating world, here are some of the most helpful things I've learned—from friends, from mentors, from personal experience, and a lot of trial and error . . .

FIRST, GET CLEAR ON WHAT YOU WANT.

Nowadays, my friends and I talk a lot about relationships. Recently, we were discussing how the first step in finding the right relationship is coming to terms with what you want. Do you want to settle down? Are you looking for something casual? Do you want to sow your wild oats? Do you want more time to work on your own goals? It sounds simple, but sometimes we don't stop and take account of that. If you don't know what you're looking for, how will you know to recognize it when you find it?

THEN, BE CLEAR WITH EVERYONE ELSE.

It's important to know what you want, and it's just as important to be up front about your intentions. If all you want is a sexual relationship, that's fine, but make sure you're clear from the get-go. Transparency is huge. Everyone in the situation should be aware of what's going on so nobody gets hurt.

CHECK YOUR BAGGAGE.

Once you're clear on what you want, get in touch with where you are right now, at this stage of your life. How are you feeling? Are you working through anything right now? Are you still healing from a previous relationship? What are your emotional needs? Mentally take stock of your situation so you don't drag your baggage into your dating life.

JUST BE YOU.

The truth is, you don't have to go out of your way to try to impress somebody. You just have to be yourself. Before a date, I don't usually get nervous. I won't worry much about it or get caught up in any feelings, because I don't like to put pressure on things. I don't really prep a lot, either—I just show up. (I once went skateboarding right before a first date.) What you get, you get. Your approach might be different, and I think it's okay to do whatever you need to do in order to show up looking and feeling your best. But remember to be true to you. Bring your realest self. After all, you want the person to like the most authentic version of you. (And if they don't, they're not the right person, and that's okay.)

PUT SOME THOUGHT INTO IT.

Before a date, think about what you want to know about the person so you ask the right questions. I always ask, "How did you get here?" Because I want to know where she comes from. What is her family like? What is she passionate about? What is she doing with her life, and what does she want to do in the future? I try to ask the same questions I would want someone to ask me. Also, think about what you want that person to know about you so you bring the realest version of you.

IT'S OKAY TO HAVE TOUGH CONVERSATIONS.

As I said, this was probably my biggest takeaway from my time on *The Bachelorette*. You've got to throw all your cards down on the table right away. Hannah and I didn't have a lot of time to get to know each other, and the next conversation was never a guarantee. I was amazed at how opening up quickly helped Hannah and me get to know each other. I told her about my past and my struggles right up front, because I wanted to make it clear to her that I had done the work and was ready for my future. I also wanted to set her up as the person I confided in.

When you're dating, I think it can be good to express yourself and share things pretty early on. I'm not saying to tell someone your entire past on a first date—in fact, specifically don't do that—but it's generally a good idea to let someone see what you're all about. We

177

all lead busy lives. I don't want to waste my time or your time. When you put all your cards out there, you can see if your cards align, and if they don't, you can move on before anyone gets invested. I try to be point-blank and simple about who I am and what I'm looking for, and I appreciate when my date can do that, too.

BE OPEN-MINDED.

Don't be quick to judge. It's good to have nonnegotiables when it comes to big things, like values and what you want from life. But also leave some room to be surprised. The right person might look different than you expect. If your cards don't line up, fine, but try not to write someone off right away or reject them based on little, superficial traits. It's okay to leave some space to learn and grow with each other. Stay open-minded.

REMEMBER, WE ALL HAVE SCARS.

Don't let someone's past intimidate you or scare you. (And embrace where *you* come from and what you've been through, too.) Hannah and I talked a lot about the idea of learning how to love each other's scars. In our lives, there are always things we're healing from. Depending on where we are in the process, some things are still wounds, while others are older and healing. If you learn how to love someone's scars—where they come from and what they've been through—then you're fully accepting them as a person. As you start to open up and trust someone, it's okay to let them see your scars, and it's good to show them that you accept theirs. Everyone has their own struggles. We need to be able to see positivity and brightness through the darkness. If you share your scars and someone looks at you differently because of it, that's not your person.

SPEAK UP.

It's important to set healthy boundaries. When you're establishing a relationship, tell the other person what you like and ask for what you want. Remember, people aren't mind readers. If something makes you uncomfortable, say so. Don't be afraid to call people out on their bullshit.

RED FLAGS

When you are first dating someone, it's easy to be overcome with excitement and to make excuses for things that don't sit quite right. Those are red flags and they are important to pay attention to, to protect yourself from a bad relationship. Here are some of the things I look for:

How do they treat the people around you?

Pay attention to how they talk to everyone. Are they polite to the server, the bartender, the Uber driver? How do they talk to their parents? If they meet your friends, do they seem interested in getting to know them? Are they kind? If someone is disrespectful, that can be a dealbreaker.

Can they have a balanced conversation?

There's this funny old country song sung by Toby Keith about a girl who talks on and on (and on and on) about herself. (If you don't know what I'm talking about, put the book down and go listen to "I Want to Talk About Me." It's worth it.)

If this sounds familiar, that's a red flag. No matter who you're out with, you don't want to sit there and have a one-sided conversation. Generally, you want to have balanced conversations, where each person has space to talk and ask questions. If someone always talks endlessly about themselves, and you continue seeing that person, you'll likely find that a lot of what they do will be geared toward serving their own interests. Proceed with caution.

Are they a vegan?

Just kidding. I have nothing but love and respect for all the vegans out there.

How do they talk about their previous relationships?

Early on, especially on a first date, I don't want to hear about your ex. But there's a time when you want to talk about your past—what happened, what you've learned, and what got you here. Pay attention to the way your date describes their previous partners. Are they overly negative? Do they blame the other person? Do they present a balanced view of what happened? Do they seem like they've taken the time to reflect and learn from their relationships? Beware if every ex they've ever had is considered "crazy."

Do they try to force or rush the relationship?

For me, that's a red flag. Sometimes, things can naturally move quickly, but I like to take my time to get to know someone as a person before jumping in full force. If your date is pressuring you to put a label on things or move at a speed you're not comfortable with, pay attention. There will be time to figure that out. Relax. Go at a pace everyone is comfortable with.

Do they try to isolate you or separate you from your friends and family?

This is a big one. If someone seems threatened by your relationships with your friends or family, that's not a good sign. Do they encourage you to spend time with the people you care about? Do they respect your platonic friendships with both men and women? Having a healthy support system is important, whether you're dating someone or not, and your partner shouldn't get in the way of that.

Do they say or do things to make you feel bad about yourself?

If a date ever puts you down, negs you, or tries to undermine your confidence in any way, that's a huge red flag. Someone who chips away at your confidence is not someone you want to be with. Anyone who doesn't light you up or bring you alive is too small for you. End of story.

Do they have outside interests?

I'm wary of anyone who has zero opinions, interests, or passions. Ditto for someone with no work ethic. I don't care what it is they have going on, as long as it matters to them. You want to date someone who has their own life. Otherwise, that puts way too much pressure on the relationship.

Did they cheat on their last partner?

If someone tells you they're a serial cheater, run. Ditto if you meet them while they're still in a relationship. If they'll cheat *with* you, they'll cheat *on* you. It's that simple.

Are they weird about their phone?

You know what I'm talking about. Do they hide it from you? Is it always facedown? Are their messages hidden? Is it constantly blowing up with names you've never heard of? Do they immediately turn it off when you enter the room? You can tell when someone's hiding something.

Do they insult people?

I always make a note of when people say negative things about other people, especially if it's meant to make themselves look better. This can be direct or indirect. For example, when a girl says, "I'm not like other girls," I notice. What does she even mean by that? What's wrong with other girls? Putting down every other woman out there is not a way to sell yourself.

Did they just break up with someone five minutes ago?

If someone is fresh out of a relationship, it makes me wonder what they really need. Do they have emotional stuff to work through? Am I going to be a rebound? It's not an automatic no, but I think it's wise to take it slow. After a relationship, I think people need time to heal and figure out what comes next, so give them the space to do that.

My favorite photo of me and my momma. This represents everything. She always had my back. She was fierce and would fight to give my brothers and me everything we needed.

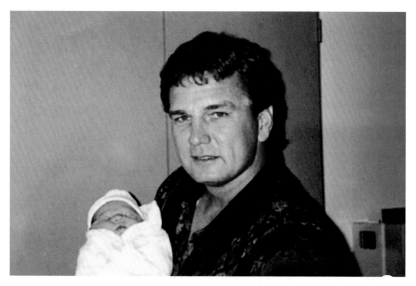

My pops. Everyone says he is my twin. Here he is holding me, his firstborn, probably thinking, *What the hell did I get myself into?*

Here is Pops again, holding on to me and a lobster. Lobstering is something he taught us, and we love to do it every year.

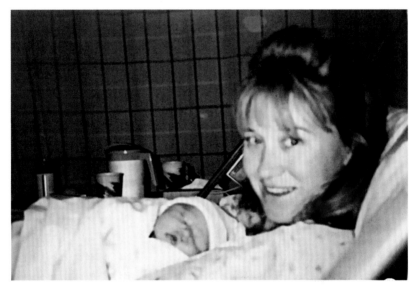

Momma holding me when I was born, oblivious to all the craziness I was going to put her through in the following years.

Another great picture of Momma and me. I have this framed by my bed. This was an event my mom put on for a local foundation. She always gave more than she had to others.

My momma just being beautiful as always. She loved to send us selfies. She was always a beam of light.

This picture of me and Momma is something I'm proud of. It shows the growth that came after I was released from Wake Forest and started playing football at FAU. I came to a new school, cleaned up my act, became the team captain, and was Student-Athlete of the Year.

My momma and me after I ran the New York City Marathon. She got to put the medal on me when I crossed the finish line and she started crying, telling me how proud she was. That made me want to cry, too, but I needed to hold it together because I had to go do an interview on TV right after.

Pops and I after the NYC Marathon. Without him, I would never have the drive or the determination to accomplish such feats. He's instilled grit and hard work in me and my brothers.

Momma, Pops, me, and my middle brother, Austin, tailgating at Ryan's bowl game.

My youngest brother, Ryan, after running his first collegiate play at FAU and winning his first bowl game. FAU is the school my momma and I both graduated from. Now Ryan always brags that he has more bowl wins than me. I never won anything in college.

Here's another photo I love. Momma was the maid of honor in her sister's wedding. She started to break down and cry while giving her speech. Without hesitation, my brothers and I got up and stood behind her. It wasn't planned, it was instinct. She is always our rock, so it was time to be her rock.

This is from our first family trip together after my mom passed. It was an all-out boys' trip in the West Virginia mountains. We wrecked two ATVs . . . expensive therapy but just what we needed.

My brothers. Blood makes you related, loyalty makes you family.

Keddy and I from when we played on our first basketball team together. To this day, he is one of my best friends. You hold on to the good ones.

Lee Quinn and I after winning the ACC Debate Championship. I always use this when I'm asked to share a fact no one knows about me. It makes me sound smarter than I look. Great time and an even greater friend. His back was sore after carrying me through this tournament.

Evidence of my short-lived and unsatisfactory career at Wake Forest.

Here I am trying to pick up girls one young summer at Wake Forest. I needed to lose those glasses, get rid of the tank top, and get a better haircut and I might have had a better chance. That's how you learn I guess . . .

Here I am cutting a rug at the wedding of one of my best friends, Andrew.

Ahhh, this is the photo that I sent in on my application to *The Bachelorette*. I think it did all right with catching their attention.

This is Valentine's Day 2019. The day I got the call to be on *The Bachelorette*. I was working a modeling gig as the doorman for Cartier.

Are they too busy for you?

I don't care how "important" the person is, the right person can find time in their life to see you or at least to let you know they're thinking of you. If they can't find any time to be with you, they're not into you.

Do they play games?

This one's not quite a red flag, but it's definitely something to be aware of. When you first start seeing someone, are they up front with you, or are they playing games? Do they reach out when they want to talk to you? Or are they concerned with who texts first, or who texts more often, or other bullshit like that?

One pet peeve I have about dating is when women get mad if I don't text them first. If you want to talk, start a conversation. I promise I'll always do the same. That whole "who texts first" game, or trying to time your messages so you seem busy, or trying not to answer too quickly? I blame modern dating culture for this particular neurosis, but I really hope we can put an end to it. I can't deal with that stuff. Both people in a relationship should be able to act on their feelings. Honestly, I like when a woman reaches out. I always appreciate when a girl starts a conversation.

Personally, I don't play games. I've been in relationships where we play games, and it never goes well. It's cut-and-dry for me—either we're working or we're not. I don't believe in "playing it cool." I respect myself (and you) more than to sit around and play a game. There are no mixed messages. If something feels funny, then something's funny. There's no beating around the bush. If I like you, I'm talking to you. If I don't, I'm not.

Trying to guess what the other person is thinking is a waste of time. If you don't know, just ask them. And if they make you feel like you have to guess, then you should consider leaving them behind.

GREEN LIGHTS

On the other end of the spectrum, there are some things that I'm always happy to see.

They can hang.

If I'm dating someone, I like to see how they do in groups and how they get along with my friends. I want a partner who can hang with my people, who can hold her own with them. If she can't hang comfortably with my friends, then I don't know if she's the one for me.

They give off positive energy.

I like energy. I like to surround myself with the kind of people whose passion when they talk about themselves and their lives and what they do can be seen. I want to date a boss. I want to marry a boss. I want to be with someone who's proud of what she does and crushes what she does—no matter what it is. That, to me, is going to make me want to boss up even more.

They can be spontaneous.

One big green light for me is when a person is positive and curious and wants to take advantage of whatever life has to offer. When it comes to potential partners, I like someone who's flexible and able to be on the go when opportunities present themselves. I'm looking for someone who's excited to do things, who's up for trying something new or jumping into something that sounds fun.

They surround themselves with good people.

When you get to the part where you meet the important people in each other's lives, remember that a person's friends say a lot about them. When a girl I'm dating has healthy people in her life, who surround her with love and lift her up, I'm always happy to see that. (I've also had exes whose friends were the type who always gossiped, bickered, and complained. That's not good to be surrounded by.) When you're in a couple, it's healthy to maintain your individual lives and relationships, and I want my partner to have good friends and to enjoy their company.

They communicate clearly.

I love it when a woman is confident enough to tell me who she is, what she likes, and what she wants. Also, while we're on the subject of communication, let's talk about texting. Everyone texts. So many texts. If I like you, and I want to tell you something, I'll call you—I'll get everything I need out in around ten minutes, and we can make plans. Not many people call these days, but I say, don't be afraid to pick up the phone.

It feels good.

The right relationship brings you peace. It's like that feeling when you get that morning "hey" text from someone you really like. You're not anxious about what's going on. You feel seen and heard and respected. You're excited to see what comes next.

ONLINE DATING AND SOCIAL MEDIA ETIQUETTE

These days, a lot of initial meetings—probably even most meetings—happen online, through dating apps or social media. As nice as it sounds to meet someone in person, in modern dating culture, we're all so dependent on our phones that it's changed the whole game. People don't have the balls anymore to go talk to someone at a coffee shop. (They might have balls when they're at a bar, but no one wants to meet someone when they're drunk and sound like a fool.) Apps define the modern way of dating.

When I was in college, we used dating apps whenever we traveled to a new city for football. We would send all kinds of pickup lines to girls everywhere we went to see what might get a response. We'd be on the bus, and every now and then someone would exclaim, "I have a match!" when someone responded to their message. I was always against hooking up when we were playing, because you'd have to break the rules to sneak a girl into your room, and it took away a lot of the energy you needed for the game. But there were a few exceptions.

When I was younger, my dad, my brothers, and I would go on road trips, and I would use the apps to hit girls up and say, "What's cool to do in this town?" It was like my travel guide. Some people would actually respond with ideas, and a couple of times I met up with girls who were cool as hell.

My attitude around dating apps has really changed over the years. I used to be totally against them, but now I think they are a true way of finding somebody. If you think about it, it's the same as if you went out and tried to meet someone in person—you're only going to match with someone you find attractive and interesting, and the rest you can discover as you get to know them. I've seen so many success stories. I have friends who have found great relationships online, relationships that have led to marriages and kids.

So, if you're currently on any dating apps or considering using them in the future, here are some things I keep in mind.

Using Dating Apps

Post Photos of You—Just You

My biggest don't when it comes to setting up your profile is don't post group photos. Don't put any pictures on there where you're with your friends, or with your siblings, or lined up with a bunch of other bridesmaids or groomsmen, etc. It's confusing! Half the time, I can't tell who you are. It's your dating profile, so post photos of you.

Be Up Front

Trying to meet someone on dating apps is like meeting anywhere else, so it's important to communicate what you're there for right up front. Some people use dating apps to hook up. Some people want to date. Some people are hoping to find a partner to settle down with in the near future. Time is valuable, and you don't want to waste anyone's time, including your own. So state what you're looking for, right in your profile. It helps to weed out anyone who has totally different goals.

Be Honest

Post photos that look like you! Not from a million years ago, not from a weird angle, not with a filter that makes you look nothing like yourself. Don't catfish people. We've all heard those stories where someone shows up for a date and the person waiting for them looks nothing like their photos. One friend recently went out with a girl who actually apologized that her photos were so old she looked nothing like them. Another friend went out with a guy, only to discover he'd since lost all his hair. Of course, I understand choosing photos that are flattering, but you want to meet someone who's interested in the real you, right? You want someone who is attracted to you and into you just the way you are. So be honest.

List What You Want

My friend has this story. She was on an app, and she kept going out with all these guys, but she had a hard time finding someone she connected with. At the time, she was seeing a therapist, and the therapist suggested she do a little experiment. "List exactly what you want—all the qualities you're looking for in a partner—right there in your profile," he said. This seemed a little forward to her. But because it was an actual doctor telling her to do this, she agreed. After she did it, the quality of her dates improved! It got her closer to finding someone who was compatible. And a little while later, she met her current boyfriend. There is a moral to the story: Don't be afraid to list what you're looking for. How can you get what you want if you don't ask for it?

Be Funny

My number one tip for reaching out to people on social media (or dating apps . . . or anywhere online . . .) is you've got to be funny. You're grouped in with a bunch of people, so you have to find a way to make the other person smile. What's going to separate your DM from someone else's DM? Make them laugh. Whether you're a guy or a girl, humor always works. In this, too, make sure you're being your authentic self. If you tell a joke that makes *you* laugh, and it makes the person you're chatting with laugh, then there's some compatibility there.

Follow . . . Your Heart

When it comes to meeting someone on social media, people have different opinions about when it's okay to follow someone you're interested in. This one is kind of up to you. Do you have mutual friends or connections? Have you ever met in person? Or are they a total stranger who seems cool? Personally, I don't usually follow people until after I meet them, but it depends on what mood I'm in. Sometimes I'm feeling frisky, and then I'll just follow them! Do whatever feels right to you.

Be Careful What You Put Out There

Nudes are a no-no. For guys, this is rule number one: Don't send dick pics. Ever. Never ever. This one is so important I'm going to say it again. *Never send a dick pic.* Everyone I've ever talked to about this (guys and girls) seems to think that dick pics are pretty much the worst thing ever.

No matter who you are or who you're into, you shouldn't have to get someone's attention through a nude. If that's what it takes, you're not setting yourself up for a very healthy relationship. Likewise, if someone you just started talking to is asking you for photos, it's a bad idea.

You have to listen to your own comfort level. Some people feel okay sending photos and some people don't want to, ever, and that's fine. Just be careful what you put out there! The internet can be a scary place.

Just Say Hi

Don't be afraid of rejection. I know, it's easier said than done. But if there's someone out there who seems cool and you think you'd like to get to know them, why not send them a message? If you're never going to see them anyway, you might as well take a shot. As my dad says, "You can always go and then come back, but you can't always go." You'll never know if you don't try!

Beware of Endless Messages

I try to stay away from too much small talk before I can meet someone in person, because I want to get to know them for real–for real. If I DM somebody, it's to say, "Hey, here I am." I'll try to make her laugh. If she responds, great. Then I try to figure out a way to meet her. Use apps and social media as a way to get your foot in the door, but once you've done so, ask them out. If you meet and it's good, *then* you can have small talk. But save the small talk for later.

Curb Your Expectations

Personally, I'm bad at this one. My friends will tell you: I'm known for saying, "I think I've found my wife," before I've even met someone. (My friends constantly make fun of me for this.) But the reason I feel like I haven't succeeded with social media dating is because I naturally build up these expectations and assumptions based on their photos and whatever their profile says. But I'll be the first one to tell you, that can be very misleading. Photos are curated to show only what that person wants you to see. What you get online is often very different from what you get in person, so never let yourself assume you know who someone is until you really meet them. Don't fall in love (or write them off) until you meet in person. Come in with no expectations. When you first meet someone, you need to figure it out from the ground up—you owe it to both of you.

Be Kind to Yourself

Remember that social media is tough. Online dating is tough. Any kind of dating is tough. It's hard to be successful at these things, so go easy on yourself. If you're struggling, trust that you're just getting closer to finding the right thing. If you're no longer having fun, take a break. Remember that you're learning more about yourself and what you want. And with each wrong date, take some comfort in knowing you're one step closer to the right one.

A WORD ON ROMANCE

We've talked about meeting people, but what about when you're in a relationship with someone? Sometimes, in long-term relationships, romance can take a back seat to the everyday concerns of life. But little things can go a long way to keeping that fire going.

When I'm in a relationship, I can be a pretty lovey-dovey guy. Sometimes it can feel scary, but whenever I've done something romantic and seen how happy it made the other person, it has always been worth it. There was the time Mariah and I had dinner on the boat. Or the time I decided to turn our regular movie night into something special. I didn't have any money then, but I took a bunch of little steps that didn't cost much. I had so many candles burning it was a full-on fire hazard. It took me fifteen minutes to light twenty-eight candles, which I'd placed all over the room. As a final touch, I had music playing when she arrived. She came in with the biggest smile. And it made the night so special.

I think romance is making the person you're with feel like they're the most important person in the world. It's making someone feel loved. We all need to feel like we're special and cared for. I get so much pleasure and find so much happiness in seeing other people smile, which is one of the reasons I love the idea of romance so much.

Romance can be over-the-top cheesy if you want, but it doesn't have to be. It also doesn't have to be expensive. It just has to be effort. A romantic gesture can actually be pretty simple—it's anything that's thoughtful and from the heart. If you need some inspiration to bring a little more romance into your life, here are some ideas to get you going:

- Tell someone they're beautiful.

- Reassure them if they've been worried about something or expressing feelings of insecurity.

- Let them know you appreciate them. This goes for big things, like telling them how important they are in your life, and also for little things, like letting someone know you appreciate the small, everyday actions they do or words they say that make your life (or the lives of people around you) better.

- Plan something. Take them to their favorite restaurant or prepare their favorite meal and light a couple candles. Go on an overnight getaway. Remember, it doesn't have to be anything grand or expensive. The cheaper, cheesier things are often the most heartfelt. Go have cheese and crackers and crack open a bottle of wine on the beach or in a park.

You'll have more fun than you will sitting in a fancy steak-house.

- Do something chivalrous, like opening up the car door. You could even do a small thoughtful thing, like washing the dishes, making the bed, or doing another chore or errand without their asking, to make their day a little easier.

- Write them a note and leave it somewhere you know they'll find it. It doesn't have to be an epic love letter—it could just be a little note that says you're thinking about them.

- Look into their eyes and think, *I'm so lucky to be with them.* And then express that. To me, that's romance.

8

FEMALE FRIENDS
AND BROMANCES

The Importance of Friendship

I'll be the first to tell you: yeah, I spend a lot of time with women. And guess what? That's not going to change any time soon.

The truth is, most of my best friends are women. I love talking and going out and spending time with them. I'm comfortable with them. I hang out with women just as much, or maybe more, than I do with guys. Yes, all those girls you see me out with are just my friends. They help me see the world from a female perspective. They make my life better, as good friends do, and they also help me to become a better person.

I don't have sisters, but girls and women were such an integral part of my growing-up experience. When I was in high school, my mom was more of a best friend than a parent. Everyone always said she was the coolest mom. She was such a strong, dominant figure in our house, but she was also so fun and loving. My brothers are the same way I am; they have lots of platonic female friends. I think, because we had such a great relationship with her, that helped us to naturally see other women as potential friends.

Two of my best friends are Katie and Mollie, both of whom I've known since I was in seventh grade. They're my voices of reason. When I was a freshman, I tried to kiss Katie on New Year's Eve. We spent the night watching *High School Musical*, and at midnight, I went in for a romantic kiss right as the ball dropped. Instead, Katie gave me a peck of a kiss and told me, "Never again."

No matter how much we try, men will never completely understand what a woman's experience is like, what kind of challenges she faces, and how she is treated because of her gender. But my female friends help me be more open and aware. They've taught me to be more sensitive to how women think and feel. They also give me dating advice and help me decipher when someone isn't into me or when I should give someone another chance. I talk to them about what happens with people I'm dating, and they'll weigh in when I need guidance. I still have a lot to learn, but my friends help to educate me all the time.

Often, I think the best way to understand where someone is coming from is to try to put yourself in their shoes. I'll never fully understand how it feels to be a woman or what women go through, but I try. And not just in the emotional ways, but also in the self-care and beauty rituals that women are told they have to undergo. That's why you'll see me getting manicures and pedicures with all the girls (I'm serious). I've also tried waxing. My female friends talk to me about *everything*. Take birth control, for example. Guys aren't often exposed to the reality of how badly birth control can affect a woman's body. If it weren't for talking about these problems with my female friends and with previous girlfriends, I wouldn't know how much women are asked to endure, while guys are allowed to be relatively unbothered by contraception. It's just one thing on a long list of responsibilities that women have that men take for granted.

Sometimes, there's nothing that teaches you more than literally standing in someone else's shoes. I participated in an event called Walk a Mile in Her Shoes, where I walked a mile in heels to raise awareness about sexual assault. It might sound like a small thing, but how else could I know how *awful* (seriously, awful; you ladies put those damn things on every day?) high heels are. And how much discomfort society expects you to go through to meet ultra-specific beauty standards.

Back home in Florida, a bunch of us will have game nights at Katie's house, where we hang out and play games and have fun. One night we played Never Have I Ever, and we talked all about sex and relationship stuff. A lot of the answers were surprising! Even after so many years together, I always learn so much from spending time with them. The more you hang out with women, the more you'll hear about what's going on in the world and what you're missing right in your own backyard. No matter who you are or who you're attracted to, having platonic relationships with members of the opposite sex helps you expand your viewpoint.

I have straight guy friends who say, "I don't have one girl who's a friend." That's bullshit! How do you expect to learn anything about women? How do you expect to expand your own views? To all the guys out there: if you don't have female friends, you're really missing out. And I would urge you to think about why that is.

Like I said, my brothers are the same way—they have tons of platonic relationships with women, and they all hang out at the house together. That's just the way we are.

Of course, just like with romantic relationships, it's important to be open and honest about your intentions at the start of platonic relationships, too. Sometimes, I'll misread what I think is a friendship, and that can get me into trouble. If a woman hits me up—someone who I want to get to know as a friend but with whom I have no interest in hooking up—I try to be clear from the beginning that I don't consider our hangout a date. It might be slightly awkward to do, but it saves you from an even more awkward situation happening down the line.

For everyone, I think being friends with women is an important step in learning how to look at *all* women with greater understanding and respect. When I'm into a girl, I naturally regard her the same way I do Katie and Mollie. I hold them in such high esteem and love who they are in a full, human way. I want to care for them and stick up for them and protect them, because I know they do the same for me. I have so much respect for them, and I would never treat any girl less or any different than I treat my friends.

In my limited experience, groups of guys, especially the ones I know, spend their time talking about three things: work, sports, and whoever at the bar they think is hot. A lot of the men in my life want to talk about macho stuff—sports, how many tackles this player got, what's going on with their job or career. It gets even worse when you talk to a lot of guys at once. Ego gets in the way. But what I've come to understand is that talk like that, all of that posturing, it's more about their insecurity than anything else. It's okay to open up to other guys about how you feel. It's okay to talk about your relationships.

Of course, that isn't the case with all guys, and there are great things about a bromance, as well. A good bromance involves someone you enjoy being around, who you know you can trust. In the best of cases, you feel comfortable opening up to them, and talking about your issues. For the longest time, I'd never been one to lean on people or share my deepest feelings with them, but since being on *The Bachelorette*, I've learned that opening up is important. Hiding things is never good, and when you hold your feelings inside, they build up until they burst. That's how you can wind up hurting people. It's always better to communicate something in the moment.

Matt James is one of my best friends. He and I met at college, at Wake Forest. I graduated high school early, and he was a year older than me, so he'd already been at school for a semester by the time I got there. He immediately took me under his wing and showed me the ropes. My first weekend in North Carolina, he took me out and we had one of the craziest weekends, which bonded us right away. We just clicked immediately. We trained together, we hung out at school, and I always liked him. But we got really close once I made the move to New York, after college and after I was cut from the Ravens.

I first started traveling to New York for modeling, and as soon as I told Matt I was coming to town, he was like, "Dude, come stay at my place." At the time, he lived in the smallest apartment in New York City. It was a three-bedroom split among three roommates, but we spent most of our time in his tiny room. The whole thing was probably the width of a queen-size mattress. He had a lofted bed— he slept in the bed, and I slept in a beanbag underneath him. But it was more than enough for us. We both loved being out in the city and having adventures, so we didn't care about having a nice apartment. We had some of the greatest times together.

Matt always took care of me. I didn't have much money to begin with, and he made my transition from Florida to New York that much easier. He's so charismatic and great at connecting people, and he helped me make friends all over the city.

Aside from his being an incredible friend, one of the many things I appreciate about Matt is that he's really motivating to be around. He's driven and successful and always finds a way to give back. He's a trailblazer in a lot of ways. We talk at least a couple times a week, and I love that we can laugh and be funny and also be serious together. We have conversations about what we're looking for and what we want, and he challenges me to aim high on all those things. I know I can talk about anything with him, and we can really get into it.

Matt is an inspiring presence, and it's always nice to have him around. If he gets up to work out, I'm like, I better get my workout in, too. We give each other accountability. If there's one thing I've learned when it comes to friendships, it's that you've got to have friends who make you better. Your people are what make you. I like to surround myself with people who are positive, who bring good light and energy to the situation. I have that in Katie, and I have that in Matt as well. I think he sees the world in a similar way to me—he really values getting out and doing something instead of sitting around the house, and he's always trying to help the community. He's one of the most generous, charitable people I've ever met.

It's important to surround yourself with friends who want you to grow. You want a circle who can push you, educate you, and help you learn. I also appreciate friends who can be a voice of reason. Someone who can call me out on my bullshit but also tell me when I'm doing well.

Just like you deserve the best from romantic relationships, it's just as important to have quality friendships, too. Eric Thomas says that your relationships will either make you or break you. They either inspire you to greatness or pull you down in the gutter. It's that simple. Iron sharpens iron—you can do so much more when you have good people around you. The people you surround yourself with say a lot about you. And that goes for *all* your closest relationships, especially your friends.

My friends these days are all trying to make a difference, for themselves and for others. I can't do what I used to do, which is hang out with people who just go to bars. That's not my lifestyle anymore, so that's not what I want to surround myself with. It's only natural that as you grow and change as a person, your closest relationships will evolve as well.

To me, part of what makes a good friendship is that we don't need to be in each other's ear 24/7. In all my best friendships, we can pick up when we see each other. For me, the friendships that don't really work are the ones in which one person needs constant attention, and if they don't get it, they complain that we don't see each other or talk enough. My friends know I'm there for them if they need me, and vice versa. But people handle friendships differently. Some people want to talk or check in with each other every day, but that's not what works best for me, and I try to be open with my friends about that.

Friendships are just like romantic relationships, in that you need to ask: Am I adding value to them? Do they add value to me? Is there a give and take by both parties? If it only goes one way, then that's not a healthy relationship. I think sometimes, people have a hard time letting go of friendships that aren't positive. Sometimes I think it's even harder to identify a toxic friendship than it is to identify a toxic romantic relationship. We've all been there.

Maybe the friendship was never balanced, or maybe it used to be good and turned toxic. You know those friends who are always a mess. They always have drama or emotional needs. They need you to baby them or take care of them, but then when you need help, they're nowhere to be found. Maybe they need to always be the life of the party. Maybe they need to be the hot one or the wealthy one or the popular one. Maybe they make everything all about them. Maybe your friendship is totally one-sided, with a friend who takes and never gives back.

If you experience any kind of success, and your friend acts jealous or pissed off, that's not a true friend. Your friends should want the best for you. Your success is their success, and their success is yours.

The first thing to look for when it comes to friendships is the nature of your conversations. Are you gossiping? Are you bickering? Are you just talking about other people the whole time? Do they only talk about themselves and never ask about you? Do they complain the whole time? When you hear somebody always complaining and bickering, that's a sign that they're hurting your emotional well-being. Help them if you can, but know that there is a limit to what you can give. You need to surround yourself with healthy people; otherwise it's going to drain you. It doesn't have to be a big thing or a dramatic fight. Over the years, I've quietly separated myself from people who weren't healthy to be around.

On the flip side, pay attention to the people with whom you can have great conversations, and fight to keep them in your life. Can you talk about things that are important? Do you challenge each other? Do your friends hold you accountable? Do they seem genuinely interested in how you are and what's going on in your life? As I've gotten older, I've become more conscious of the quality of my conversations. I don't spend time with people who talk about nothing.

My mom used to have these friends I couldn't stand. I could always see that she was the ultimate friend to everybody. Her friends would call on her for all kinds of help and emotional support, and she would be there in a heartbeat. But when she was down and out, those same people were never there for her.

But on the other hand, my mom's relationship with her friend Angela was one of the healthiest friendships I've ever seen. They were two people who loved each other, looked after each other, and wanted the best for each other. It was so pure. In Florida, we experience hurricanes all the time. Every time a hurricane was coming through, my mom would be there, putting the shutters up at Angela's house before it hit. She didn't even need to ask; my mom just did it. They knew they always had each other to lean on, and I know that their friendship helped both of them get through some very tough times.

A true friend is always there, no matter what. If you need emotional support, if you need a shoulder to cry on, if you need someone to celebrate with, you know they'll be there. They lift you up when you're down and try to set you up with the best possible outcome. They put a smile on your face. They bring you positive energy. When someone has good energy, you just know. You feel it. Some people are just happy to be near you, and that kind of positivity is infectious. Seek out those people and hold on to them once you've found them.

For years—eight years to be exact, starting our sophomore year of high school—my friend Katie was in a bad relationship. Her boyfriend hated me and would never let her hang out around me. He was an insecure guy, and he was threatened by my friendship with her. Katie and I were just homies, and he had nothing to be suspicious of. But he didn't understand the friendship we had.

Soon after I broke up with Mariah, Katie and her boyfriend broke up, too. We made a pact that we had to stay single for a year. We promised each other we would take that year to reflect on what we'd learned, focus on loving ourselves, and have the most fun we could, all while being on our own. We went on trips, we went out boating, we talked a ton and took care of each other. I learned so much from her that year. It was a great example of friends supporting each other through a dark time and lifting each other up.

Once we were both in a healthy place again, we decided it was time to start dating. Now she has a great boyfriend. I'm a huge fan because I can tell how supported he makes her feel. She's so happy, and he's secure enough to give her space to live her life. They respect each other and give each other their freedom, including valuing their individual friendships.

Now, having good friends I love and trust is more important than ever. Out of necessity, since I entered the spotlight after *The Bachelorette*, my circle has gotten smaller. Since the show, everyone is always coming out of the woodwork to hit me up. People I haven't talked to in years suddenly want to be my friend again. When your life changes like that, right away, it's natural to become extremely guarded. It's hard not to develop trust issues when you don't know why people want to be around you.

People are also weird. Soon after the show wrapped, I rolled out of bed and went to meet one of my homies for breakfast at my favorite local hole-in-the-wall spot. A guy I went to high school with was also eating there, and he took a really zoomed-in photo of me with my hair looking all crazy. He then posted it to his social media, saying, "Tyler looking rough at breakfast this morning. It looks like the show didn't end well for him." I was like, *What?* This was someone I knew pretty well. To my face, he'd been super buddy-buddy, but then behind my back he posted gossipy shit like that? He was trying to get attention by posting about me, and it felt like a breach of trust. It taught me a lesson early on that I was no longer just Tyler to the people around me.

These days, there are also people I can't hang out with because they're a liability. In the past, I didn't have anything to lose, and I wasn't overly concerned about how my friends reflected on me. But now there's a lot on the table. I can't risk having people around if they could put me or others in a bad place. They might leak something or act inappropriately.

I learned in high school that you need to be careful and that you might be held accountable for a friend's actions. One time, I almost got arrested for a buddy's pot and steroids. I had nothing to do with the drugs, but because we were friends, people assumed I was involved. I was never even a part of that, but just being around him nearly got me into a ton of trouble. It's an important lesson for all of us: you need to be smart about the people you call friends.

But with all that said—even though there will be people in your life you grow apart from, and others you might actively need to move away from—you should try to never burn bridges. I always keep it cool, because it's better for everyone to be that way. There's no hate in my heart for anybody.

Before I wrap up this chapter, I have to mention my very best friend of all.

I think the only thing that can ever resemble the kind of unconditional love God has for us is the love our dogs have for us. You could be gone for two weeks or two hours, and your dog will give you the biggest kiss when you come back regardless. My dog, Harley, has helped me through so much—depression, disappointment, heart-break. I can just grab her and hold on to her and lean on her when I need to, and she can just lean on me. Are you familiar with the five love languages? I think my strongest love language is touch. To be able to hold my dog at the end of the night, when she comes to lie on my chest and I can breathe a little deeper—in those moments, I know that as long as she loves me, everything is okay.

That's the mark of a good friendship. You can be completely your-self with them, and they make you feel comforted and supported. Sometimes you might disagree, but you know that you can solve it.

Girls, dogs, Matt. The greatest friends.

That's the kind of unconditional love we all deserve.

The Real Tyler:

ACCORDING TO HIS FRIEND KATIE

I first met Tyler in seventh grade, and then in ninth grade, he came over on New Year's Eve. I have two older brothers who are super protective, and that was the first time Tyler came to our house, so my brothers both waited by the front door for him to arrive. They're kind of short, and Tyler's obviously very tall, so they greeted him, but they couldn't really intimidate him, so that was that. The rest of the night, we hung out in my room watching a movie, and at the point where the characters kiss, Tyler tried to kiss me. I gave him the quickest peck in the world and was like, "What the hell are you do- ing?" Ever since then, we've joked around with each other about that. I put him in his place quick.

Now, I just say I have another brother I never asked for.

It's true that he loves to hang out with us girls, and it goes both ways. In general, having a guy friend at girls' night is the best thing in the world. Typically, we talk about boys, and we love having Tyler offer his input to everything we say. It's so funny but also so eye-opening. I used to read into so many situations, like, "He must be playing hard to get." Then Tyler weighs in and says, "No. If he's into you, and he's worthy, he's not playing games."

Tyler's definitely the goofball of the group. He takes everything over the top. If we're doing karaoke, he's breaking out a full-blown dance routine to go with it. It's never half-assed with him. He has two feet into everything, all the time.

In high school—and in general, because he's carried this through to today—he would insert his name into any R&B song out there. So, for every Usher song, Tyler sings his name wherever their name is. It's annoying, but it flows, so it's funny.

When it comes to hanging out, he's so adventurous. We'll just pick up and do things, 24/7. I wasn't always used to that. I dated someone for eight years who didn't get along with Tyler, and when I was with that person, I got so used to constantly just chilling at home. Then when Tyler and I started getting close again, I'd answer my phone, and he'd be like, "Hey, Kate, I'm outside. We're going somewhere." And then we would. He's always ready for the next adventure, and it pushes me way out of my comfort zone.

In our generation, with social media and everyone constantly looking at their phones, it can be hard to get people's attention and even harder to know when they're listening. But when I talk with Tyler, I know he's listening. He looks at me, he gives me advice, he tells it like it is, he holds me accountable. It's so nice to have someone just hear me. He knows everything, and I would never question whether I can trust him. We talk about whatever problem I'm having, we fix it, and he'll never talk about it with anyone else.

During college, Mariah was his first serious girlfriend. There were other little ones here and there, but that was the first time he was in a real, long-term relationship. I think—and I'm sure he would say the same—he wasn't in a good place himself at that time, so he wasn't able to treat her the way she deserved. It was a spiral effect.

When they broke up, I finally got the nerve to break up with my long-term ex, which was overdue. That first night, Tyler and I, and another friend of ours who had just broken up with her boyfriend, went out together, to this place where they let you tape dollars to the ceiling. (Very classy!) We wrote on our dollars, "Single Society," and made a pact that we would both stay single for a year, until we were hopefully ready for a relationship. We told ourselves it was our mission to figure out who we were and what we liked, outside of what other people wanted us to be.

That year, we did anything and everything—we went out on the boat, took night cruises, had dinner at each other's houses with our moms. (We would also go to Ale House like it was actually our job, so I definitely gained five pounds during our "journey.") The worst part of breaking up with anybody is that once you're bored, you want to fall back to what's comfortable. I remember Tyler told me, "Any time you want to text your ex, text me." That was our thing. He recited his number out loud until I memorized it. Any time I was upset, I would call him, and we'd find a way to keep busy. It was a good time. And it still is!

Tyler calls or FaceTimes everybody—he is *not* a texter. When FaceTime came out, I think it made his life complete. Everything is a FaceTime. I was never a big caller until the past three or four years, but now I am, and it's all because of him. If he calls me and I text him back, he won't even respond.

One morning, he called me and said, "I signed up for *The Bachelorette*," and I laughed but didn't think anything of it, because it's one of those things where everyone applies but no one actually gets on. When he got on the show, I *still* didn't think much of it, because not everyone who goes on the show blows up. But then he did.

At first, it didn't feel any different. It was cool to see my friend on TV, but it was still just Ty on TV. And then, when he first came home, we went to mini season in the Keys, for lobstering. That's where it hit me that he was as big as he is, because I played photographer the entire time we were there. Any restaurant we went to, everyone would ask if they could take a picture with him, and of course he always says yes. And every time, they would just hand me the phone. It was so funny, and also weird, because to me, he's just Ty. When we're not out in public getting photo requests, he's exactly the same and everything feels the same as it always has. Fame has not changed him at all.

The hardest thing is that I can't respond to the people who spread rumors or say mean things about him. I'm not a confrontational person anyway, but when you see somebody you respect and love so much have their name trashed by people who don't even know him, it's frustrating. People make assumptions too quickly. I wish everybody had the chance to meet him, because then they would be like, "Oh, crap. Kid's genuine." Because even if you don't want to like him, you're going to. Even when I'm pissed at him, I still love him. He just has that effect on people. He definitely made my life better, and I think anyone who meets him would agree.

We have this pact that when we both get married, he's going to wear a dress and be my maid of honor, and I'm going to wear a tux and be his best man. When we first made the pact, I remember saying, "You won't actually wear a dress! That will just be for funny pictures." But he insisted that he's going to wear it for the entire wedding, and I know he will. So, if I ever get married, that will be something to look forward to.

There are a lot of things to love about Tyler. I think the first is that he's so genuine. He's extremely motivational. He doesn't let anybody around him settle. If I'm a teacher, then I need to go ten steps more and be the best teacher. He's constantly pushing all of us, in a way that's awesome. Also, he's just goofy! I love his goofiness. He's just a big old genuine goofball—that's pretty much it.

9

WHAT I'VE LEARNED
FROM REJECTION

That Time I Got Broken Up

with on National Television

Rejection is a necessary part of life. Some of the best things in my life—new directions, new relationships, and a lot of growth—have ultimately come after being rejected. Still, just because rejection is inevitable, just because it can be an opportunity for growth, doesn't mean it's fun.

I've experienced a lot of rejection, but so far, only one happened on national television. The truth is, during my time on the show, rejection was the furthest thing from my mind. All along, I just wanted Hannah to wind up with the right person for her. I hoped that it could be me, of course, but I mostly wanted her to do whatever would make her the happiest. When it got to the point in the show where there were just three of us left—Jed, Peter, and me—I could relax a little, because I felt sure that whomever Hannah wound up with, at least it was going to be a good guy. (Of course, this was be-fore I knew Jed had an off-camera girlfriend, but that is another story.) Hannah eliminated Peter, which I know was super hard for her. And then there were two.

Jed and I both had to go pick out an engagement ring, which shocked me back to reality. It made everything real in a single second. I had no idea what to pick. I asked the designer, Neil Lane, "What do girls like? What's cool right now?" I looked at the producers, I looked at the guy, I looked at the rings. I'd think I had picked one, and then they would put another one in front of me. In the end, I just picked the biggest one. That thing was huge. I figured, Hannah's a loud and proud person, so this is her ring.

The night before the final day, I stayed up all night. I spent hours working to memorize my proposal speech. This was Hannah's big day, and I wanted it to be amazing. Completely perfect.

I never did get to say that proposal to Hannah, but here is what I planned to tell her:

Hannah Brown—from the moment we met, you've captivated my soul.

You started this journey saying you're not looking for perfect, you're looking for real. And I can say with all honesty, our relationship has been the most real thing I've ever had in my life.

I always had an idea about the man I wanted to be and I knew I'd get there. I just didn't know how. Then I met you. I realized to become the man I was meant to be took you pushing me to be that person. I've grown emotionally, spiritually, and I'm madly in love.

The most precious things aren't found in the simplest of circumstances— a rose, while beautiful, can be wrapped in thorns . . . but it's embracing the thorns that lead us to a love that can last through anything.

Hannah, I know our love was slow to start, but it's a light that will burn forever. I know you had a label on me from the beginning, but these are the only labels I want: husband, best friend, lover, protector, father to our children.

The moment I started falling in love with you was dancing with you in my arms on our first date. When I looked into your green eyes I just knew that . . .

Like a ship without a sea
Or a song without a melody
I don't know where I'd be or what I'd do
'Cause I was made for you.

I'm so madly in love with you. I want to support you in your dreams and make you happy for the rest of your life. I've given all of myself to you—will you give all of yourself to me? I know we always say, let's have a day . . . but let's turn this day into a life.

Hannah Brown, will you marry me?

That night, I kept listening to the same song on repeat—"Beyond," by Leon Bridges. (Great song.) "Don't wanna get ahead of myself," he sings. "Feeling things I never felt." It felt like the perfect soundtrack for this moment. When I finally got in bed, it took me a long time to fall asleep because I was too excited. I got maybe two hours of sleep.

In the morning, I woke up and I immediately started rambling, still reciting the proposal over and over again. I took a shower, and as I stood under the water, realizing the weight of what was happening, I got super nervous. I was so overcome with anxiety that I actually started dry heaving.

I gave myself a moment to calm down and put on my nicest blue suit. By the time I was dressed, I was over my anxiety and filled with pure joy and adrenaline. I remember holding on to that ring, thinking, *Holy shit, this is about to go down.* I wanted to nail it, for Hannah. I remember standing in that villa in Greece, looking out at the blue water, trying to take everything in. Without question, this was the biggest day of my life so far.

As I got closer to seeing Hannah, I got more and more excited. Once I got in the car, my nerves left. It was go-time. There was no turning back. This was a commitment I wanted to make—to go for, to fight for. I was ready for the next level.

I sat in a restaurant and ordered food and coffee while I waited, but I felt too nervous to really eat. As time ticked on, I couldn't help but draw conclusions. It was taking so long that I figured there must be a breakup going on. As the delay got longer, the more I felt like things must have been on my side.

Finally, it was time for me to go see Hannah. I felt excited. I felt happy. I felt like I had finally made it happen. I'd reached a point in my life where I could be the best man for Hannah and do what was right by her. I couldn't wait to take this big step, in both of our lives.

I arrived and went to see Chris Harrison. Throughout the show, some of the guys would kiss his ass, but I wasn't really like that. One time we were in the gym together, and I thought, *The last thing this guy wants to do at the gym is have to talk to one of us.* So I didn't bother him.

Anyway, Chris said his thing, and then he walked me up to Hannah. And then it was time. By this point, I'm big cheesin'. I couldn't control my smile.

When I looked at her, I immediately noticed that she looked distraught.

Oh, she's just nervous, I thought. *Everything is okay.* After all, this was such a huge thing. It was perfectly normal to be nervous.

I started going through my speech, feeling good, thinking, *Oh, I got this*. As I'm hitting my lines, she said, "Stop, stop, stop." Then she looked down and started shaking her head.

Oh, shit.

That was when it hit me.

I said, "This ain't it, is it?"

"I love you," she said, "but I love someone else."

I was upset, but something came over me right away. It was a voice that said, "You're hurt, but this isn't about you. This isn't your day; this is her day. Make things okay for her. Make it easy for her. Get in the car. It will all be okay." If I truly believed in what I'd said all along—that this was her journey—that meant this was also the final chapter of that story. I wanted to do whatever I could to help her enjoy the moment. So that was what I did.

If you watched that final scene, then you saw me try to suck it up.

"I have so much love for you, and I'll be your biggest supporter," I told her. "You and Jed are going to be great together. You guys are going to be amazing."

And I truly meant it.

(Again, at the time, I didn't know he was two-timing all of us.)

It was clear she was upset and that this was a tough conversation for her. But this was supposed to be the most amazing day of her life! I wanted her to feel good and to have confidence in her decision. What she had to do was tough. She had finally reached the end of this journey, and I just wanted it to be the best for her.

After the fact, Hannah and I talked about that day, and she completely misunderstood my reaction. She thought the fact that I acted like it was no big deal meant I didn't care, that my heart wasn't in it. So in a way, I *did* help her feel better, but not in the way I meant to.

We said goodbye, and then I finally got in the limo. I felt broken. It took all my effort to hold it in. Once I got into the car, I started to let go a little bit. But I still felt so shocked, I wasn't ready to let myself break down.

I wasn't upset with Hannah. I wanted her to do whatever was best for her, and whatever would make her happy. I was upset *about* Hannah, of course, but it was also bigger than that. When I got dumped on the show, the first thing I said to myself was, "I've always gotten *this close*." I was *this close* to making it in football, I was *this close* to winding up with Hannah on *The Bachelorette*. I was always able to make it just within reach of my dreams, but I was never able to close the gap. I felt disappointed and exhausted.

During my time on the show, I formed relationships with all these people on the crew: the cameraman, the sound people, the producers. My producer was crying, because she knew how badly I wanted this. When I finally got out of the car, my cameraman told me, "You're a champ. This is the hardest part of the job, and you've handled this better than anyone I've seen. You're going to do great things." He gave me a huge hug. That's when I finally got choked up.

Afterward, I went through the hotel, down through the resort, and stood, looking out at the water. When I saw the ocean and the mountains stretched out before me, that was when I finally started to sob. I may have held it together until after the cameras were off me, but once I let it go, I cried and cried.

I felt tired of being *this close* with everything I'd done. In that moment, it seemed like I was always coming up short. I ordered some food and tried to chill out.

I was alone again. I was heartbroken. I had no choice except to mourn. For the rest of my time at the hotel, I licked my wounds in private. I grabbed a couple beers, got in the bathtub, and listened to Juice WRLD's *Goodbye & Good Riddance*. I must've listened to the whole album three or four times, just screaming it out and letting it all go. Being alone, hearing those songs, singing those lyrics, I came out knowing I would be okay.

All I wanted was to just go home and hug everyone. I wanted to see my family and friends. I remember, at one point, I was at a restaurant and I started to cry, right there at the table. I was so overwhelmed, all I wanted was to be back with the people who love me.

From the second I got my phone back, everyone in my life was calling me, asking, "What happened? What happened?" But I was careful never to say anything at all.

In my first few days back at home, I thought about everything that had happened. *What have I learned from all this? Why do I keep coming up short?* That was no way to live. I needed to figure out what I was doing, so that I could make the changes that would enable me to take it all the way.

I missed the first episode of *The Bachelorette* because I was on the plane home when it aired. But I caught the rest of the season, and I found it all pretty entertaining. Watching it after the fact, and knowing how everything wound up, was like watching someone else— Young Tyler, a version of myself I had already grown out of. I kept looking at that person and thinking, *Oh, if only you knew what I know now.* I mostly just laughed at myself—and if I look back at it now, I still laugh. In a way, watching the show felt like freedom. I felt more and more free each week, because once everyone else knew what happened, I didn't need to hide it anymore.

Rejection isn't easy. But if we take the time to reflect on it, rejection can teach us a lot. As I headed back home, I thought about all the times I'd been rejected before this and what those experiences could teach me. As much as that shit stung, as much as it hurt, I was used to it. I've always dreamed big. Occasional rejection comes with the territory. I learned from a young age how to deal with it.

When I left the show, I immediately remembered getting dumped by my first girlfriend, Emily, in seventh grade. I remembered getting cheated on by Kelsey when I was in high school. After that, I'd thought, *Screw relationships.* After those early heartbreaks, I was determined never to be rejected again. My heart became hardened, and I became the ultimate party boy. I decided never to date anyone, because I didn't want to get hurt. I wouldn't learn until later that that wasn't a productive way to deal with rejection or a healthy way to consider relationships. Now that I was older and wiser, even though this heartbreak aired on national television, I wasn't going to react in the same immature way.

I remembered playing football—first at Wake Forest, then at FAU, then trying my hardest to get recruited for the NFL. I thought about getting called in and then cut by the Ravens—again and again. All those rejections stung, but they taught me something. And each one made me stronger.

When I got cut from the Ravens for the final time, it put me in a deep, dark hole. All that stuff added up. Playing in the NFL had been my dream, and then suddenly, it was clear that it was never going to happen. It led to my rock bottom, but also to my greatest transformation.

Don't get me wrong, Hannah's rejection, her telling me she

wanted someone else, that shit hurt all on its own. It was a thousand punches to the gut. But the reason I cried afterward—the reason I felt absolutely wrecked—wasn't only because of heartbreak. I was tired of coming *this close* with everything. It was the accumulation of years of rejection that I hadn't totally processed and moved past.

It all goes to show you that you can't run from rejection. I ran from the pain I felt from my failed relationships. I ran from the pain I felt when I got cut from my college team and then from the NFL. But my feelings caught up with me eventually, and then I had to process them all at once. I think the best thing about rejection is that it puts you where you're supposed to be. You can't ignore it or escape it. You can try, but it will catch up with you in the end.

Sometimes, even if you give yourself the space to reflect, the pain that comes from rejection can last a long time. After I got cut and I saw all my buddies playing football, all getting their big breaks while I was sidelined, it killed me. I was happy for them, but I thought I should be out there, too. Just this past year, I went to the Super Bowl and I almost cried. I had to take a moment, away from everyone else, to stand there, looking out at the field and getting a grip on my emotions. I felt like I was supposed to be there—not as a spectator, but out on the field. Even all those years later, I couldn't help but feel like I let myself down.

But thinking about what might have been if I had made it to the NFL also reminded me of all that's happened because I didn't. I thought about all the new paths to come my way and how grateful I am for them. And I remembered how I can't let everyone—me, my agents, my family—down by not staying the course.

Out of every experience I've ever had, rejection is the one that's helped me grow the most. In every case, it forced me to reflect on my role in why things turned out the way they did. Why is this happening again? What did I do now? And that reflection made me who I am today.

These days, I've learned how to do a self-check on myself. *Why did this happen? What did I do, and what could I have done differently? Is there something I can do better in the future?* If I find that I fucked something up, then I try to learn from it. If I find that it was out of my control, then I accept that and move on. Rejection teaches you how not to fuck things up again. After it visits you, you can't give up. You can't stop. You have to put your head down and put one foot in front of the other. There can be beauty in rejection, especially if you're willing to keep working hard. New opportunities will open up in ways you couldn't predict.

Some things just aren't in your cards. But I've learned there's always a silver lining. Sometimes, things don't work out a certain way so that something better can happen. You can't always see that while it's happening, so you just have to trust that something great is coming around the corner. As cliché as it is, it's just one door closing so another door can open. There's that saying, "Rejection is God's protection." When you get rejected from something that wasn't meant for you, it might save you from a bad situation—a nightmare boss, a bad relationship. Other times, it's so that something better can come along. Rejection may seem like a dead end, but it's also the birth of something new.

Personally, when it comes to dating, rejection is a huge fear. It's scary! Nobody wants to be rejected by anyone; we all just want to be loved, you know? With all my talk about facing rejection, I think I'm still battling this one just like everyone else. Rejection in relationships is extra hard, because it can feel so personal. I'm fearful that

I'm not enough. I'm afraid of losing anyone else. I don't want to bring someone in, only to wind up saying goodbye.

But I still want to open my heart to people. And that's probably the biggest lesson that rejection has taught me. It's bad, but it isn't the worst thing that can happen. The *worst* thing you can do is nothing. The worst thing you can feel is regret. I'd rather give it everything I have and get rejected than spend the rest of my days wondering, *What if . . . ?*

Even if you've had your heart broken, even if you're scared shitless, if you don't take a shot, think of all the good things you'll miss out on. You'll regret not meeting someone, not talking to someone, not getting to know someone, not opening up and giving it your all. Avoiding regret is worth some rejection.

If something doesn't go your way, don't let your ego convince you that it's a bigger deal than it actually is. If you believe in yourself, if you're confident in who you are, if you know you're a good person, that's what matters. That's what defines your worth. You don't want to be with anyone who doesn't appreciate you.

As I've gotten older, I've found that I've also gotten tougher. Rejection is kind of like fear in that way, where the more you face it, the less you'll feel it. Rejection gives you scars, it gives you tough skin, it gives you strength. It makes you a badder mofo than you were before, as long as you do it right. My greatest rejections have given way to some of my greatest opportunities. And that's how it goes. If you face your rejection, learn what you can, put your head down, and keep on trying, good things will come.

The Real Tyler:

· ·

ACCORDING TO HIS FRIEND
AND MENTOR ROBB

What Tyler and I have is like that big brother/little brother re-
lationship. It's always full disclosure, everything on the table. I'm a
little more than a decade older than him, married with a family, and
those are things he wants, so I think for him it's like a crystal ball into
the future. We talk about girls, settling down, what he's looking for,
what he's not looking for, what to watch out for. We talk a lot about
commitment and how, if he makes a commitment, he wants to honor
that. We also talk about life stuff, like finances and playing the long
game.

I call the Camerons the Pirate Clan. Jeff, Tyler's dad, is the orig-
inal pirate. He's like me—an old salt; a real, authentic Floridian.
When you trace our ancestors back, they lived and survived off the
natural resources in Florida. (If my granddaddy were alive and knew
people paid for water, he would fall down dead.) When you find
people who see things like you see them, that's a bond.

Tyler and his brothers, Austin and Ryan, are the three pirate boys. They are true guys' guys, rambunctious boys. Like the time when they parked the boat in the living room—that's just a Tuesday at the Cameron house. Their boat (naturally, I call it the pirate ship) is this beat-up boat that's been sunk to the bottom of the ocean, and they brought it back up. They're living. They're not being coddled, in any way.

When Tyler backed the family boat through the front window, at first there was a lot of cussing from Tyler's mom, Andrea. But then there was also this smirk, like, "These are my boys." I saw her make that face so many times. Always because someone tore something up or did something stupid. Those were her boys. Theirs was such a special relationship.

When I first met Jeff and Andrea, they weren't together. But they had such a true love bond. That's so rare and so unique, and I watched firsthand how they were with each other. They weren't together for their reasons, but they truly loved each other. When Jeff got sick, Andrea, no questions asked, just took care of him. Her boyfriend understood. It was such a beautiful dynamic. The love, the bond, was so strong.

One Christmas, we all did dinner together. Andrea cooked a prime rib, Jeff came, and it was like we were all just one big happy family. Afterward, my wife and I talked about it, like, "*That's* what love looks like. They're not together, but that's real love." Andrea nurtured him. It was always really beautiful to see. They would fight like wildcats, but they loved each other.

Some people get divorced, and there's tension you can cut with a knife. With them, they would be at football games together, and it was fine. There were some really cool lessons there. What's really important? People. Family. That's true love. Nothing else really matters.

When Tyler first went on *The Bachelorette*, my wife asked, "Do you think he's gonna do well?" and before it ever started, I knew he would. His life prepared him well for that. He's been in high-level locker rooms. He's been the leader in the huddle. That prepares you for these moments. I think the instincts you saw on the show had everything to do with that.

My favorite moment of the entire show was when that Luke guy was being ornery, saying everyone better lay their hands off him, and all of a sudden, Tyler said, "Or what?" As Big Brother, I was like, "Hell yeah, Tyler! Hell yeah." I was running around the house with my chest pumped out, I was so proud of him.

Tyler shares everything with his friends—and I mean everything. I stayed at their place in Jupiter once, and for one thing, these dudes get up at the butt crack of dawn. At 5:30 a.m. people started coming in the room. First Tyler comes in to get something in a drawer. Then five minutes later, Matt's in the room, grabbing a shirt. Then five minutes later, his friend Brown Bear's in there, rummaging around in the same dresser, grabbing some clothes. This just kept happening until everyone had finally gotten dressed. In his house, they all share everything. Tyler, Austin, Ryan, Jeff, Matt, Brown Bear . . . if you go look at all their Instagram pages, you'll see them all, at some point, wearing the same outfit. It's like if one of them has a shirt, it's a communal shirt.

I've never seen Tyler have an ego trip. He always makes time for people. This one time, we were in the river, and these girls in another boat recognized him. They were taking pictures and tripping out, and Tyler said, "Robb, take the boat." He stood up, said, "Can I use your skurfboard?" The girls were so giddy they couldn't even speak. Then Tyler dives off the boat, swims over to their boat, jumps up on their board, and went skurfing. He skurfed with these girls for probably fifteen minutes, and everyone who wanted to get pictures for their Instagram did. He made their day.

Tyler just wants to help the people around him. Even with his friends, he's constantly like, "Use me. Tag me. If I can help you, in any way, please do it." To me, that kind of security and confidence is rare. He knows that nobody makes it to the top alone; we all need people to help us get there. He's secure in what he's doing and knows there is enough to go around.

You meet certain people who have that charisma about them, and Tyler has that. But he's more like Cool Hand Luke. He's more laid-back, genuine. He's an open book and a generous person, with his time, with everything he has. There is no greed to him. Nothing pretentious, nothing for show. Tyler is a good guy—at the soul level, in his heart, he's a good dude. That's a rarity.

10

ALWAYS BE YOURSELF

What Fame Has Taught Me

Sometimes I have to pinch myself.

There are so many moments when I stop myself and think, *I can't believe this is real.* The way my life has changed since being on *The Bachelorette*—it's just mind-blowing. When I first got cast, I thought I'd be on the show, get dumped the first night, maybe get a couple thousand followers, and then come back to Florida to chill knowing I did a cool thing and had fun with it. Instead, I'm now living a dream life. You want to pay *me* to go to Paris? I get to make money by getting in an RV and going cross country?

I get to travel to new places and meet new people. I live in a New York City apartment, on the fiftieth floor of a building that overlooks the skyline. Whenever I'm home, I look out the windows and reflect on how lucky I am to have had my life changed so dramatically. I never expected this, but at the same time, I'm trying to appreciate every second. I feel so grateful and thankful. All the time, I think, *Man, I am blessed.*

Growing up, I always thought there was going to be a time in my life when I'd be successful. I always believed it, even though I wasn't sure how I would get there or what that success would look like. Now that the opportunity is here and the time has come, I realize that never in a million years could I have believed that this would be my path. I couldn't have planned the steps that got me to where I am today.

Sometimes, it's hard to wrap my head around this new life, because I feel like I'm still regular old T.C. I haven't changed. But everything around me is completely different. When I first got home from the show, my boy Steve was like, "You didn't change one bit on the show. You were always yourself, and you still are." That was such a relief to hear, that I was still grounded after such a life-changing experience. I know I'm incredibly lucky, but I also think part of the reason good things have happened for me is because I was authentic, I was true, and I was respectful.

And here is the big promise: I'm not going to change. Now that I've come back from the show, one of the things I'm most proud of was the reaction from people who know me. My friends and family said as they watched, they saw the Tyler they knew. All along, I vowed to be myself and stay true to my beliefs and my morals. I've always been exactly who I am, and I have no plans to change that.

All of a sudden, an awful lot of people have opinions about what I should or shouldn't do. People weigh in on my dating life; people weigh in on my career. But at the end of the day, I am the only person who has to live with my decisions. I do. At the end of the day, I'm going to be me, and I'm going to do what makes me happy and helps me feel fulfilled. The same goes for dating. At the end of the day, I enter a relationship with one other person, not the entire country. So the best I can do is to be true to myself.

After the show, the media put me on a pedestal—remember that whole "Respectful Woke King" thing? Now when people see photos of me that contradicts that image, it's easy for fans to feel let down. They feel that maybe I've changed. I just have to keep reminding myself that I am not responsible for how I'm portrayed, and the only thing I can do is act in a way that makes me and my friends and family proud.

There is a business principle, the 80/20 rule, that says 80 percent of what you produce actually comes from only 20 percent of your efforts. Well, when it comes to being in the public eye, I think there's something like the 90/10 rule. Ninety percent of the way people perceive you is going to come from 10 percent of your actions. That's just the way it is. And further, no matter what you do, it's safe to assume that 10 percent of people just aren't going to like anything you do. This is true everywhere in life; there will always be people who just want to critique you. It's what you do with it that matters. For whatever reason, they've got it out for you, so there's no sense in trying to win them over.

The way I look back on my own memories is similar. For me, it's the bad things that stand out the most. Because those hard moments were outliers, I remember them more vividly than the good memories from normal days. The same thing applies to other people's opinions. The negative ones hit harder. In a sea of a million nice comments, the haters stand out the most. Let me tell you, if you allow it, that shit will eat you up. That's why you can't let it get a foothold. I'm not going to get upset because some *Bachelorette* fan who's never met me is talking trash about me on Facebook. I try to remember that it has nothing to do with me and everything to do with them. Hurt people hurt people. I've been on both ends of that one.

Here's one thing I've learned about success of all kinds: Don't drink the Kool-Aid. Don't listen to the press, good or bad. You can't buy into your own hype, or your ego will get in the way and you'll lose touch with your true motives. You can't get bogged down in the bad things people say, either. Only you know what's real and what's true. If you buy into what other people want (or what you think they want), it will subconsciously affect your decision-making and you won't be the truest form of yourself.

In some ways, I think football really trained me well for dealing with this. As a quarterback, you're scrutinized after every single play. I threw a lot of bad passes and lost a lot of games, but I learned how to not be bothered by the criticism of others. You dust yourself off and live to die another day. The trick is to keep a level head. You can't get too excited, and you can't let yourself get too low.

Speaking of keeping a level head, for the most part, I can keep my cool when I meet celebrities. I think part of the reason I don't get star struck is that when I played football, especially as I got closer to the NFL, I spent a lot of time around players I looked up to. I had to learn to relax and treat them like regular people.

There are a couple times when I haven't been able to play it cool, though. In 2019, I brought my mom as my date to the People's Choice Awards. It's a night that I'm incredibly grateful for. We had the best time. During the awards, my mom sat behind Blake Shelton and we couldn't stop smiling. It was one of those moments when I kept thinking, *What alternate universe am I living in?*

At one point during the night I went to go to the bathroom, and as I walked down the hallway, I nearly got run over by security. It was like a stampede. I looked farther down the hall to see what the big deal was when I saw . . . an angel.

She was glowing.

I looked closer, like, *Who on earth can it be?*

The angel came a little closer.

It was Jennifer Aniston.

"Hey!" she said. "How are you?"

I looked around; I was sure she must have been talking to someone else.

"Me?" I said.

"Yes! It's good to see you. I hope you're having a good time," she said. And then she continued on, floating down the hallway.

I just stood there, thinking, *I can retire now.*

A lot of people are nice, and other people are not so nice. Sometimes, people I work with will say to me, "You're so nice and easygoing and real."

I always wonder, *Who are you used to working with?*

I work hard, I show up on time, I do my best to always be respectful. I don't think I deserve a trophy for that—I believe it's how it should be—but these things go a long way in the business world. I believe that no matter what it is you're doing, good things will come if you're a good person and you work hard.

I also believe in the power of words. Before I went on *The Bachelorette*, I would jokingly say to my friends, "I'm gonna go on that show and get second place." I feel like I spoke it into existence. After my season ended, I went on a podcast with Nick Viall and I said, "Matt James should be the next bachelor." And then he was the bachelor, and the first-ever Black bachelor in the show's history. Of course, I didn't actually conjure anything up. There are a lot of reasons that Matt got picked to lead the show that have nothing to do with me saying that. But what I'm trying to convey is that when you speak things, you give them energy, and that helps to make them real.

People talk a lot about manifesting, and I think it has two parts— the first part is speaking something into existence, but the second part is hard work. They say the recipe for success is when opportunity meets preparation, and to me that's what manifesting is—being prepared so that you put yourself in the perfect position to make the most of every opportunity.

Say you want to play football, and you're put on the scout team. If your job is to be the practice dummy, be the best damn practice dummy there is. *That's* how you manifest. Work your ass off at every opportunity that comes your way until more doors open.

Ashton Kutcher gave this speech at the 2013 Teen Choice Awards, where he talks about exactly this. It's such a good speech, everyone should watch it. He talks about all the odd jobs he had and how seriously he took each one of them, which eventually led to his success.

Also? Put smiles on people's faces. I love when I'm walking down the hallway and I pass somebody and they have that vibe, where they're positive and they're into what they're doing and they have good energy. There's nothing better than when you meet somebody new and it's clear they're having a fabulous day. I want to know that person, I want to be around that person, I want to work with that person. *That's* how you open doors.

I love my fan base. I am so grateful for them, because I wouldn't have any of this if it weren't for them. If you ever see me out somewhere and you want to take a picture or talk, I'm always like, please come! If I can do something to make your day better, I will do it a hundred times. If I can make the people around me happy, I'm all for it. (Just not while I'm eating.) Still, sometimes people can get a little carried away—this one time I was sleeping at the airport, and someone tried to wake me up to take pictures. She tried to wake me up three times. Once I was actually awake, though, I did it. I didn't blink an eye. Without people who believe in me, who are excited to see or hear what I have to do or say, none of this would be real. And I never take that for granted.

I always think back to this time when I was a kid at a baseball game. Montreal Expos' Brad Fullmer, a baseball player who almost nobody knows, flipped me a baseball after one of the innings. I became probably one of only ten kids in the entire country who knew his name. He made my day with one small gesture, and I became a fan for life.

When I was in high school, my dad taught me it was important to thank everyone who came to see you play. I also wore these wristbands, and after every game, I would give them out to kids who watched the games, because I remembered what an impact baseball had when I was just a kid. So now, if someone wants to say hi or take a photo with me, and that might make their day better, I'll always do it in a heartbeat. No question.

There are times, though, when people can take things a little too far and it can be scary. One time, paparazzi took pictures of my house in Florida, so everyone found out where I live. Suddenly, all these people were driving by my house and taking pictures. Another time, a woman—a person I never met—flew to my house *from Hawaii* with her suitcases and a dog and tried to move in. Harley was not having it. Now, I'm a guy, and I'm a big guy, and I can take care of myself in most situations. But it made me worry a lot for other people and their safety. Trying to figure out where celebrities live, and making that information public, is crossing the line.

Privacy is important. My brothers' privacy is important. My family's privacy is important. They didn't sign up for this. People would slide into my mom's DMs and talk trash to her. She was always defensive of my brothers and me, and she felt like she had to stick up for me, but it would cause her a lot of stress. She hadn't signed up for that.

My life has changed in all these amazing ways, it's true, but it's also become harder, more scrutinized. There are so many times when I feel on edge or like I can't breathe. Sometimes, it feels like I can do nothing right in the public eye. There are days I spend struggling with massive internal battles. You get a lot of shit, no matter what choices you make. People don't like when you break from expectations and it can be hard to look past the criticism. People complain that I'm not still doing construction. People complain that I'm not dating Hannah Brown. (Even though Hannah didn't pick me!) And there's nothing I can do about that.

While we're on the topic of Hannah, though, there is something more that needs to be said. At the end of the show, after everything about Jed and his offscreen girlfriend came out, Hannah asked me out again. Now, to be clear, she is the one who reached out to me. Later on, it was framed by the media and the tabloids like I was the one who pursued her and that felt unfair. Of course, I was glad to hear from her, and I was happy to see her again, but I also made it clear that I needed to take some time for myself to figure out what was right for me. After all, no matter what my feelings were before she turned me down, my feelings had changed, naturally, after she sent me home.

Hannah and I made plans to see each other, but I didn't totally comprehend how major the reaction to that would be. We saw each other in L.A., where yes, I slept at Hannah's house, but we didn't sleep together. We weren't in a relationship at that point, and we definitely weren't boyfriend and girlfriend.

Two days later, I was seen in New York City, out on a date with a different girl.

Now I know, this was a major mistake on my end. Not because I shouldn't have been dating, because I was very clear with Hannah all along that after the way the show ended, I needed some time and space to figure things out. I even called Hannah in the afternoon the same day I arrived in New York and told her again that I thought we both deserved to date other people.

But I still put Hannah in a tough, tough position.

I want to be clear that I never went out with anyone to upset Hannah. My knucklehead brain truly didn't realize what a big deal that would turn out to be. I was still completely new to fame, and I naively didn't consider that anyone would care who I was seeing or what I was doing. I definitely didn't realize people cared enough to take photos of me, this guy who didn't know anything about anything, and then post them in the news. Before all this, I thought paparazzi took photos of people like Brad Pitt and Angelina Jolie. I didn't think they took photos of the reality show runner-up from Jupiter, Florida. I was like, "I don't have any real talents! Why are you taking photos of me?" After the story hit, everything became totally different. I had a lot to learn. My world went from being small to being enormous.

• • • • •

Anyway, I honestly didn't realize that the whole thing would blow up. I didn't realize Hannah would need to go through all these interviews fielding questions about my dating life and explaining how she felt. She handled it well; she answered everything with class. But that's one thing I feel very, very sorry for. If I could go back and do it all again, I would handle it differently. My communication should have been better. I just didn't yet understand how this celebrity world works.

Back in the day, I would date people until something stuck. For most people, that's how dating should be. You go out with someone, you talk and get to know them, and when you find a person who agrees that things should move forward, that's exactly what you do. But that's not how things go anymore. Now, I try to remain as private as I can. I've seen how fans and the media can lash out at people I date. I don't want there to be any outside pressure—on my date or on me—when we're trying to figure out how we feel about each other. Plus, I want to form my own opinions of someone and not be influenced by whatever's being thrown at me.

So now, I try to avoid dating in public places, at least at first. Until we feel comfortable, I try to stay behind closed doors or do things at off-hours. As much as I'd love to be out in the open from the beginning, keeping my personal life private feels like the best way to give a new relationship a fair shot. It helps take the pressure off— if we make it that far, then we can play the game and see how we do under pressure.

Trying to figure out your relationship amid all the pressure of the outside world sucks. They say I'm a player if I take a date out for pizza. But isn't that what dating is? Going out with different people and getting to know them, to see who you ultimately want to be with? I'm trying to get to know these women, as people and as friends. But I'm not a regular guy anymore, so I can't date like one.

Trolls make everything hard. They try to dig up every nasty thing or find every bad photo. They'll dive into someone's past and drag up old stories or things they've done. Rationally, I know that if somebody is making a burner account to troll me, a person they've never met and likely won't ever meet, what that person has to say should not affect me. But still, it subconsciously bothers me. If you read the wrong message, it can really ruin your day. So now my policy is to block all troll accounts immediately. Why would you want those negative thoughts in your life? There are so many times I want to write back and defend myself or engage with whatever they've sent, but I try to remember, if they're saying mean things about a person they've never met, chances are, they're in a hurt place and I don't need to make it worse by tearing them down. I've got a big voice now, and I want to use it for better and more positive things than that.

When I got home from the show, my brother showed me Reddit, including all the subreddits dedicated to *The Bachelor.* That site is a truly endless well of content. I read the praise, and I was drinking the Kool-Aid. But when I stumbled across horrible posts, they weighed on me heavily. It started to affect my decisions, where I might stop myself from doing something because I'd wonder what people would say. I've learned that that's not okay. You can't hold back on doing the things you want, that feel true to you, because you don't think others will approve.

I try to hide a lot of things from the internet, but somehow, the internet always knows. The sleuthing can be pretty damn impressive. Recently, someone saw a hand in one of my photos—a hand!—and figured out who I was with.

The world of celebrity comes with enormous stakes. If I make a mistake now, it's a big deal and can have a real impact on my life and the lives of my friends and family. People look at me from the outside and think everything looks great. (And a lot of the time it is great! I'm not going to lie, and I'm not taking for granted all the amazing opportunities that have come because of my newfound fame.) But there are still a lot of things you don't see. I still go through the same difficulties as before. I still experience those same human struggles as anyone else. Life is still life. People pass away. The girl I like still doesn't like me back. And when you factor in fame, and the million pieces of bullshit that come from it, it can feel like a lot to manage. We all have our own struggles, no matter how shiny someone's social media feed looks. You really never know what they're going through.

It's especially hard being in the spotlight when you're facing a personal trauma. When I lost my mom in 2020, her death made it difficult for me to trust people, because I don't want to lose anything else. It makes it hard to open up and let people inside. And let me tell you, when you're having a hard time under a spotlight, it can make everything feel magnified.

Still, the positives outweigh the negatives a zillion to one. My dad always says, "Get down on your knees and pray and be thankful." And I do. I feel grateful every day. Right now, I would rather be doing what I'm doing more than anything else in the world, and I plan to chase it for as long as I can.

Before the show, I rarely had more than forty bucks to my name. I was always struggling. The fall before my mom passed, I was able to have my family up to New York City to have Thanksgiving together—my dad, my mom, my mom's boyfriend. It was incredible to have the means to make that happen. When my mom suddenly passed, I was able to tell my brother, "Buy the first flight out. Here's my credit card." I also bought my cousin a flight so we could all be together. After my mom passed, I was able to take care of her house. I'm able to support my brothers and help them pursue the things they want to do.

People always ask me what's on my bucket list, but the first thing on my bucket list is to help my dad knock off whatever's on *his* bucket list. I want him to experience everything his heart desires—hunting, fishing, seeing the world, whatever he wants to do. My dream is to make that happen. The part where I can provide and take care of the ones I love is the best thing to come from all this. I am forever grateful and indebted to the people who support me. I couldn't do any of it without them.

I don't know what the future holds. Who does? For now, I just want to have fun. I want to do things with the people I love, because that's what matters most to me. I don't pursue anything because it's cool or because somebody has a big name, because that's not authentic. If my friends and the people I care about can find success working on projects together, nothing would make me happier. I love that I get to make videos with Katie and my homeboys, where we can act ridiculous. I think when you put something out there that comes from the heart, and when you genuinely enjoy putting it together, that translates. Before any of this happened, my dad always said, "You're going to do whatever you want to do." That was true then, and it's still true now.

That's one piece of advice I have for whatever path you're on:

When you get an opportunity, do what *you* want to do. Do what excites you. Do the thing that lights you up. Do what makes you happy. And do it your way. People will either love it or hate it, but you need to do whatever it is you're about. That's the only way to make it authentic, and that's what makes something stand out.

The only thing that is certain in life is that things change. I know enough to recognize that everything has a shelf life. As much as there are parts to fame that I don't care for, I'm going to give it a run for all I've got and make the most of it while I'm here. I'm going to take every opportunity that's put in front of me. I'm going to enjoy this while it lasts, and then one day, when things inevitably shift back out of the spotlight, I'll move on to the next part of my life. I'll finally settle down and coach that football team. I'll move back by the water in Jupiter, to share a life with my friends and family. And I'll look back on this crazy time in my life with total gratitude and awe.

If I can help my community, have a family, and spend a bunch of time with my kids, that's the goal. The thing I've always wanted most is to be that parent who's able to be around their kids all the time, teaching them and helping them grow and having fun together. No matter what, though, I will always try to do my best and lead with love. Whatever the future holds, I know I'm going to get there by putting one foot in front of the other, just taking it one step at a time.

The Real Tyler:

ACCORDING TO HIS BROTHER AUSTIN

*In high school, Tyler used to be a little bit cocky, but he's defi-*nitely humbled himself since he hung up the shoulder pads. He went through all those adult realizations, about how work sucks and things aren't as easy as they look. Before he went on *The Bachelorette*, he was working with my dad doing construction. I remember he would come home every day, covered in dirt, wearing these boots that were filthy. He would be exhausted to the point where he could barely keep his eyes open. He's got one of the strongest work ethics I've ever seen. I've never witnessed anyone who has as much consistency. He is the living, breathing example of setting goals and continuing to work on them until they become reality.

For a long time, Tyler wasn't the person who would sit and talk about his problems. We came from a household where we were taught you don't sit there and cry about something, you do some-thing about it. We didn't share our struggles or our feelings, but after going on the show, he's much more in tune with his emotions. It definitely changed him, in that it forced him to open up and be true to himself, and that was a very surprising thing to see.

If I ever have big pressing questions about anything, I can ask him, and he'll give me straight-up answers. He's always been extremely supportive of my relationships. Back when I was in high school, he took my girlfriend at the time out for pizza, just to get to know her better. I wasn't even there—I was working out or training or something—but he went out of his way to make time for this person who was important to me. I really appreciated that.

When Tyler said he was going on *The Bachelorette*, I didn't know much about it. When the publicity photos got released, people in my ROTC program (mostly girls) would come up and ask me about him, and I got a better idea of what the show was about through talking to them. Still, I didn't realize how serious anyone was about it until I saw him on the show. I wasn't sure what to expect, but when I saw Tyler and the way he was acting around Hannah, I was like, "He's going fucking gaga over this girl." With him, you can tell how he feels about someone by the way he looks at them, and he was definitely into her. Even with all the changes in his life, Tyler definitely hasn't changed at all. (And if he ever did, then Ryan, my dad, and I would give him shit about it.) He's still just Tyler.

Last year, on the day before my birthday, my brother wanted to take me out to celebrate. We went to a restaurant, where these two girls noticed him. The next thing you know, they come up and are like, "Are you Tyler?" and did the whole usual thing where they freak out for a second, then ask him why he's here. One of them turned to me and said, "I don't know who you are, but I'm sure you're famous, too." And I was like, "Yeah, I'm a SoundCloud rapper." I like to pretend I'm famous and mess with people in that situation; it's one of the funnier things about it. But any time a random person comes up and asks him for a photo, Tyler will go out of his way to talk to them and take a picture with them. He's always willing to do whatever he can to make someone's day better.

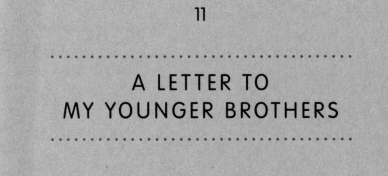

11

A LETTER TO
MY YOUNGER BROTHERS

When I first sat down to write this book, I envisioned it as a letter to my younger self and to my younger brothers, filled with the lessons I've learned in my life so far. I wanted to save them from some of the troubles I'd encountered along the way, and for them to know they are worthy, valued, and loved, for exactly who they are. With that in mind, it seems like a fitting way to end the book is with an actual letter, to my brothers and anyone else who needs to hear it.

· · · · ·

Austin and Ryan,

The first thing I want you to know is that you'll make mistakes— that's just part of life—but when you do, try to learn from them. When you make a mistake, the goal is to not make it twice. In life, just like in football, you have to learn and grow, and then keep on moving. It's like that John C. Maxell quote, "When you fail . . . fail forward." Mistakes can help you get back on the right track. So take them in stride, learn from them, and then go. If you dwell on them, they'll kill you. If you sit on them, they'll kill you. In two weeks, I promise those mistakes won't seem like such a big deal.

When it comes to dating and relationships, communication is everything. You can't assume the other person knows or understands your thoughts and feelings. Be up front about your intentions. If you want to be something more, that needs to be known. If they're on that shit, they're on it. If they're not, then you need to respect how they feel.

If you enjoy spending time with someone, see it out. See where it can go. And if you don't enjoy being around someone, be honest about that, too.

It's tricky, because I know we've grown up in a hook-up culture. It's okay to hook up, but always be respectful. Have good intentions. Ask the right questions and make sure that both of you are comfortable. It's important to be transparent.

Tough conversations are hard to have. It's hard to be vulnerable. It's hard to say things if you know the other person may be hurt or disappointed. But try to remember how you would feel if you were on the other end. I've been dragged around, and that's not fun. Save them the time of worrying and trying to figure out what's going on and just be up front.

When I was younger, I saw hooking up like it was a hunt, a chase. But let me tell you, from someone who's done it, that's not fulfilling or sustainable. What's fulfilling is finding someone you love, respect, and care about. Find someone whose company you enjoy, a person you like being around, a person you want to share your secrets with, good and bad. That's what's real.

I wish this were a given, but don't ever push somebody into something they don't want to do. If they're hesitant—even in the slightest—then it isn't happening. When it's not right, it's not right.

In every situation, without fail, treat every single girl and woman you encounter with respect. In a perfect world, girls need to feel strong and comfortable enough to communicate what they want, but you play a role in that, too, because you need to give them the space to speak up.

When I was in college, I tried to be cool and macho. I let my ego lead the way. Fuck that. Be exactly who you are. Be weird and cool and fun and flamboyant—be whatever you want to be, as long as it's true to yourself. I know I've told you this before, but I really mean it: you're so much cooler than cool if you just be yourself.

As it turns out, real strength isn't the macho kind. Being masculine and strong isn't about how much weight you can lift or how many girls you can hook up with or how much money you can bring home. It's not about how many beers you can shotgun or crack over your head (Ryan). It's about how you can be mentally healthy. You can have conversations that are tough, honest, real, that cause you to be vulnerable. I think being masculine is being someone who's able to care for others. So sometimes put yourself aside and take care of those around you.

Do fun things for the people you love. It's okay to show affection and to show you care. It's okay to listen. It's about doing the little things that make someone feel like they're the most special in the world.

Remember, the grass is always the greenest where you give it water. So when you find something good, take care of it.

I think everyone struggles with being present, but you have to make the most of every moment. So as my coach always told me, be where your feet are. Be present. Enjoy this moment—no matter how great things are or how hard they seem. Take every moment for what it is and see where it can take you.

Say "I love you" to anyone you love, as much as you can. Tell them any time you get a chance, because you don't know when it's the last. Even if someone knows that you love them, it's always nice to hear it.

Learn as you go. And remember, you only have to take it one step at a time.

You've done great so far. But keep going. I can't wait to see what you'll do.

Questions & Answers

· ·

Your Questions, Answered

I get a lot of questions from people, especially on Instagram. One thing I've learned from reading them is that, man, y'all can be savage! Some people ask some pretty dirty things, too. But a lot of you come up with really good questions. Thank you so much for taking the time to ask. I've done my best to answer some of my favorites here:

Q. What's your favorite emotion?
A. I like that feeling when you're really, really hungry, and you finally get some food, and you're so hungry it makes you do a little happy dance while you're eating. But on the real, I guess it's when you're in love, and you're very intimate with someone and feel a true connection with them. Is that cheesy? Is that even an emotion?

Q. Which is the real you, the perfect gentleman on *The Bachelorette* or the wild child you are now?

A. No one's perfect.

They're both the real me. I've always been this fun, outgoing person. I was that way on the show, too! You saw some of the most intimate moments, one-on-one dates when Hannah and I discussed the big questions. Those are important conversations in any relationship, especially one as serious as mine with Hannah. Of course I was a gentleman, on my best behavior. Now, you see the rest of my life, too, 24/7, and you don't get to see my dating life anymore, because I keep that private. So it makes sense, that's how it would appear. But I've always been both of those people. I like to have fun. I try to always be that guy who has a blast, enjoys life. But I will still hold the door for you, take care of you, and always respect you. These days, you're basically seeing me on a different TV show, which is my life through the lens of Instagram. The angles are different. The person is the same.

Q. Is settling down and marriage something you want?

A. Duh.

Q. What is your biggest dream? What do you want to do, as an end game?

A. I want to live on the water in Jupiter, with my wife and a bunch of kids. I want to coach high school football and do everything I can to help kids get to college. That would be my dream come true.

Q. If you could have one superpower, what would it be?

A. I'd teleport. First, I would teleport everywhere in Florida. I mean, everywhere in the world. I know there is life outside of Florida. And then I would teleport to a bank vault (just kidding). I don't know why people would ever pick flying or X-ray vision or invisibility. No. You want to teleport! It's obviously the best.

Q. What's your favorite TV show?

A. *This Is Us.* It makes me so emotional. I'm behind right now and need to catch up. But I love it.

Q. If you could only watch one movie for the rest of your life, what would it be?

A. *Hitch.* I say this because in college I didn't have cable, but I had four DVDs, and *Hitch* was one of them. I fell asleep to it nearly every night.

Q. What's your biggest pet peeve?

A. What grinds my gears is when I FaceTime or call you, and you *text* me a reply. If someone does that, we're going to fight.

Q. How did you deal with the loss of your mom? Do you have any advice for someone who is grieving?

A. It's hard. You have to take it one day at a time. It hits you in waves; you feel strong some days and completely weak the next. When my mom passed, I surrounded myself with people I love. Sometimes doing that would create a distraction, and that was helpful. Other times, I just needed to be alone. Losing someone is almost like going through a breakup, where all you want to do is call that person, but that person is gone. So whenever I got that feeling that I wanted to call her, I would call my friends. I would lean on them and do stuff with them and let them be there for me. I know my mom wouldn't want me mourning, because she was always the life of the party, so I tried to keep that in mind.

If you're going through a loss, surround yourself with people you love, and also take some days or some hours or whatever it is you need to sulk a little bit. Be by yourself and let it hurt. I would go on therapeutic car rides where I would listen to music and cry and cry. Now, whenever I see a butterfly or a clear sky, I think of her. That either makes you smile, or it makes you cry, but it's beautiful either way. Remember, a heart that feels broken is that way because it also felt loved.

Q. How has your journey with loss changed your perspective on living?

A. Losing my mom really showed me how important it is to enjoy life. It felt like it happened in the blink of an eye—one minute she was good, and the next she was gone. Now, I always think, life is precious. Life is short. A lot of things are outside our control, and it's up to us to make the most of whatever time we're given. You just never know what life has in store. My mom was supposed to be the coolest grandma. I'm always conscious of how I need to cherish the people I love and make the most of the time I have. I don't want to get to a point where I blink and discover the years have passed me by and I have nothing to show for them. I also make sure to tell those I love that I love them.

Q. What's your favorite memory with your mom?

A. I have so many good memories, but my favorite is probably seeing her at the finish line of the New York City Marathon in 2019. It was a huge accomplishment I got to share with her. At the time, we were both struggling with the growing pains of being in the spotlight, and this was one time when we didn't worry about that and took the time to celebrate and enjoy being together and caring for each other. All my life, she was always such a sports mom, but by that point, I hadn't played for a couple of years, so to get to relive that moment with her, and have it connected to a huge athletic accomplishment like that, was amazing. I'll never forget her crying on me, and me holding back the tears because I had to go on TV. The night before, we had this huge dinner with me, her, all her friends. I also got to show her my first real, adult apartment. I didn't have any furniture yet, and still she was rearranging things, making boxes into furniture for me. She just crushed that stuff. That was one of the coolest weekends ever. That hug with her, at the finish line, is something I'll never forget.

Q. How do you stay so positive and happy after going through such a difficult loss?
A. I still have my dark times and my difficult moments, I definitely do. But I put on a smile, even sometimes when I don't want to, because there are other people around me. I have to make sure I smile so my little brothers can smile. If I were to be down and negative all the time, it would bring down the people around me. So I chin up and show the people looking up to me that it's okay to take on the world. I also know that's what my mom would want. Positivity breeds positivity. I hope that my going out there and showing I can still push myself shows other people that they can, too, even if they're going through hard times.

Q. What are your greatest strengths and weaknesses?
A. I'd say my biggest strength would be that when I'm committed, I'm committed. Whatever it is—my training, a project, a person—I'm

an effort person. If I'm doing it, you're going to get everything from me.

My biggest weakness is that I can't say no. I'm too nice, and I don't like confrontation. I'd rather avoid conflict, so too often I say yes and just take something on, even if it's not a good idea for whatever reason. Then I'll wind up taking on way too much and overburdening myself. I'm getting better at it, but it's still a struggle.

Q. What's the first thing on your bucket list?
A. Whatever's on my dad's bucket list! I'll start working on mine once his is done.

Q. What's your favorite thing to do with your dad?
A. Going fishing. Going out on the boat. Having an adventure.

Q. Would you rather burp farts or fart burps?
A. I'd rather fart burps. Wouldn't everyone? I would hope so.

Q. How do you deal with anxiety?
A. The best way I've found to deal with anxiety is to do something that completely disconnects me from the rest of the world. For me, all my anxiety is generated by my phone, whether it's trolls, emails, my bank account. So when I am feeling anxious, I pick an activity that will take me out of my phone and make me engaged and focused on what's in front of me instead. It could be basketball, wakeboarding, even scuba diving, because nothing else matters when you're down there underwater. I find group, active hobbies work the best for me, because they put me in a totally different frame of mind. Any time I can move around and connect with people in a real way makes

me feel better. When I get a really good sweat in, whether it's a long run or playing basketball, I usually stop afterward and think, *What was I tripping about? It wasn't that important.* No matter how upset you are about something, just think: five days from now, two weeks from now, a month from now, a year from now, it'll be water under the bridge, and you won't care.

Q. How do you get through a breakup?
A. That's a good one. Here are my rules for breaking up:

Remove all photos.
You must remove every single photo with the person from your social media. They need to be gone. Gone! No one will know the market is open if that market is flooded with signs of the past. Remove all the photos. No excuses.

Out of sight, out of mind.
You can't possibly move on if you keep seeing what the person is up to all the time. Do not check their social media; that's a recipe for disaster. If it's a cordial breakup, you can mute them. If you mute them, at least you won't see them anymore, but you can avoid that text reading, "Why'd you unfollow me?" If it ain't cordial, you need to unfollow.

Call someone else.
Whenever you start thinking about your ex, call your friends. Do not, under any circumstances, reach out to your ex. Call someone else. If no one's around, get busy. Getting busy is the most important thing.

Move on.

Oftentimes, this might mean dating other people. But only you will know when you're ready.

Q. How has being on *The Bachelorette* changed your life?

A. It's changed my life completely. It's given me a platform I can do good with. It's given me financial opportunities, to be in a better position to take care of my brothers, to take over my mom's house, to help my dad out. Without these opportunities, when my mom passed, we would have been screwed. It's given me the chance to do things I love and also to impact people down the road. I get to travel the world more and do fun things. The opportunities have been so incredible, and I'm so grateful for it all.

Q. Have you ever truly been in love with someone?

A. Yes, twice. With Mariah and Hannah.

Q. Are you shy around a woman you find attractive?

A. Yes and no. It depends on the kind of vibes we're giving off. But if it's someone I'm really into, I definitely take things super slow.

Q. What's your worst date story?

A. Honestly, it was probably the Amsterdam date on *The Bachelorette*. The date card read, "Get ready to ride off into the sunset," and I was like, "Fuck. This probably involves horses." As I've said, I do not fuck with horses. But this date was hard for more reasons than just the Clydesdale I was expected to ride.

I get there, and I remember immediately thinking, *There better not be horses.* And surprise! The next thing I know, I was looking at two massive horses.

I was supposed to be following Hannah around this beautiful city, but I was in complete panic mode, squeezing this horse to death with my thighs. The date was already not going well. Then we went to try food at this stand. She gave me a pickled herring, and it did not sit well. I didn't think it was possible to feel even *more* uncomfortable on the horse, but now I did.

Hannah was like, "It seems like something is bothering you." I told her, honestly, there was nothing wrong, other than the whole horse thing. But she kept pressing. The more I said nothing was wrong, the more Hannah got mad at me. But truly, nothing was wrong! The more she asked me, the more upset I got. There was a lot going on at that time with Luke, and I suspected that she wanted me to open up about the situation with the other guys. But I didn't want to spend time on our date talking about drama if I didn't have to. I think she felt I was holding something back from her and it just kept building up tension between us.

Now, everyone was mad—Hannah was mad, I was mad, the horse was *definitely* mad. When the night portion of the date came around, Hannah *really* kept trying to get me to open up. She kept pushing me to say things I didn't want to say—about my family, about my life growing up. I didn't have anything to hide, but I didn't want to make a pity story about myself on TV or to throw my family under the bus. Plus, I wasn't in a mood to be emotionally forthcoming after having a really stressful day.

Luckily, Hannah understood where I was coming from, and she

gave me the rose. But she told me later that while we were in the heat of it, she considered sending me home that night. I remember when I went back to my hotel room, I felt so beaten up and defeated, it was like I'd fought twelve rounds with Evander Holyfield. I may have gotten a rose, but all I wanted was to go to bed!

Q. What's been your favorite thing about spending time in lockdown due to COVID-19?

A. Spending these past few months at home, in Jupiter, was time I needed with my brothers. My mother passed away on February 29, 2020, her funeral was in early March, and our self-imposed quarantine happened right after. There were times when we would be fighting and crying, and times we would laugh and have fun. But we needed that. We were all hurting, and we had things to work out. Sometimes, you need to go through struggles or outbursts in order to come out the other side in a healthier way. We needed to talk through some dark things; we needed to see that we were there for one another no matter what. Now, I think we're all better for it.

Q. What's your favorite song?

A. "Riser" by Dierks Bentley. (Believe it or not, it's not a Juice WRLD song.) I used to listen to it before every football game. The coach would put up a highlight tape before we'd leave the hotel for our game, to put us in the zone. Then he would give us a little pump-up speech. After that, "Riser" would be the first song I listened to. "I'm a riser. / I'mma get up off the ground, don't run and hider." It's gritty. I'm always going to get out of this one way or another. That's always been my thing.

Q. How are you so carefree? I'm genuinely jealous.

A. No matter how it looks, no one is totally carefree. But I try to surround myself with people who are relentlessly positive, because that energy is infectious. I have one friend whose mantra is "No bad days," which he says (and lives) all the time. I think you are what your company is. If you have high-energy people around you, you're going to be that way, too.

Q. What did you want to be when you were small?

A. My dream was to be a big basketball star. I wanted to be the next Shaquille O'Neal. Sadly I never got tall enough for that.

Q. Would you ever go back to school? If yes, for what?

A. Yes! I would go back to study accounting. I think it's such an incredible tool. Learning to keep score of your financial life is so important.

Q. What's your worst fear?

A. I'm afraid of not reaching my potential, in any arena, whether it's being a father, a builder, a coach, an entertainer. I know when I'm at my best, I'll be able to help out so many other people. My worst fear is not being all that I can be.

Q. If you had a chance to know when and how you'd die, would you want to know?

A. That's pretty deep. But you know what? I think I would want to know. Because I'd want to know how much time I have to make an impact. If I knew I only had two or three years left, I'd do my best to spend time with the people I love. That knowledge would force me to live my life to the fullest every day. That's something I try to do anyway.

Acknowledgments

··

Thank you to Haley Heidemann, my agent, for seeing the potential for this book before I could. Thank you to Cassidy Sachs, my editor, for taking a chance on me (and dealing with me). Thank you to Caroline Donofrio for being my therapist, putting up with my shenanigans, and managing my crying. Thank you to the whole team at Plume/Dutton for helping to put this all together. This experience is something I will cherish forever.

To my dad, Austin, Ryan, Katie, Mollie, Robb, Matt, and Mrs. P: thank you for your contributions and your kind words. You guys will be receiving 0 percent of the sales of this book, but I'll take you out for a steak. Your friendships and blessings have taught me there's no amount of money that could ever make up for your presence in my life.

I also want to acknowledge Harley, for sitting on my lap and being with me the entire time I wrote this book. Adopt don't shop.

ACKNOWLEDGMENTS

I'd like to thank Hayley, Bari, and Chelsea for being my mean older sisters and great sounding boards, and for letting me know when I have stupid ideas. Thanks to Luke and Troy for hearing me out but agreeing with the mean older sisters most of the time.

Last but not least, thank you to everyone who has supported me since my time on the show. Without you guys, none of this would be possible. I hope to share many more great memories with y'all, and I am forever grateful.